Winning through Accommodation

The Mediator's Handbook

The Use of New, Alternative Methods
of Dispute Resolution in the
Last Decades of the 20th Century

W. Richard Evarts

James L. Greenstone

Gary J. Kirkpatrick

Sharon C. Leviton

**KENDALL/HUNT
PUBLISHING COMPANY**
Dubuque, Iowa

CLARIFICATION OF TERMINOLOGY

The English language does not include a singular neutral pronoun meaning *he* or *she* that is equivalent to the plural pronoun *they*. In the absence of such a pronoun, the word *he* will be used throughout this text to refer to both males and females, thereby avoiding awkward construction in trying to avoid phrasing which might be considered "sexist." Where appropriate for the same reasons, words such as *man* and *men* will be used to imply persons of both sexes collectively. The use of such terminology is in no way intended to imply masculine gender exclusively, except in those cases where the context obviously refers to the male sex.

The cover design is based on an idea by David Cohen Leviton.

DEDICATION

To the readers, our colleagues,
all agents of interpersonal peace.

Contents

Preface

At a time in most lives when communication is vital, mediation allows for the building of bridges, the defusion of hostility, and the settlement of issues. The mediation process is a mutual search for a reasonable solution; neither party can win at the other's expense. While the mediator controls the process, it is the disputing parties who identify the key issues involved in the conflict and make decisions concerning the settlement of these issues. Mediation provides a private setting for the disputants to be the authors of the resolution rather than the victims of an imposed judgment.

"When the tissue of life is woven of legalistic relations, there is an atmosphere of moral mediocrity, paralyzing man's noblest impulses."

Alexander Solzhenitsyn

Acknowledgment

The authors wish to acknowledge the contributions, insights, and encouragement of our friends and colleagues who have made this work possible.

Introduction

This book was stolen. More precisely, the manuscript from which this book is published was stolen three days before the final copy was due at the publisher.

Can the police retrieve what was lost? How long will this delay our printing? Questions, such as these, were more than a little troubling.

What would you have done? Report the crime to the police? It was reported. What next? Wait until the police called you in to identify the recovered property? That long wait might never produce the manuscript.

Immediately after the theft, one of the authors visited every convenience store in the surrounding area. At every store, each store clerk was informed of the theft and promised a reward for the return of the merchandise. Each person was told that the objective was to retrieve the stolen materials (clothing and other personal items were also stolen), not to catch and punish the perpetrator. This purpose was kept clearly in mind. Within three days the manuscript and most of the other items were returned.

The negotiating process which preceded the return of the stolen items was a great lesson for the teachers. An "informer," who may really have been the thief, surfaced in response to the reward. The manuscript was returned first. Next, the items of clothing and briefcase. The informer was told that the principal objective was the return of the goods, but that if the goods were not returned, then the principal objective would be to hunt down and punish the perpetrator. Thus, both the informer and the perpetrator, even if they were the same person, had every incentive to return the property and no incentive to keep the property. True, the reward had to approximate the value that could be obtained from the sale of the property on the street. Since the sale value is far less than the replacement cost, the author had every incentive to pay a "reward" for the return of the goods. Since the reward approximately matches the return obtainable through sale, the thief had every incentive to return the goods, provided that he could elude punishment for the theft. Ironically, it was in the interest of the authors to avoid punishing the thief.

Did the author pay the reward for the return of his own property? Certainly! Failure to pay the reward would have established a reason for retaliation by the informer. Such a failure would also have created an inequity by breaching the promise on which this agreement was based.

Some would contend that such negotiation is unprincipled. Indeed, a strong argument could be made that paying for the return of one's own merchandise reinforces criminal behavior and undermines the legal order. However, one could also argue that such reinforcement through performance of both parties might encourage the thieves to contact the victim before selling the goods on the street. The monetary and human costs of crime would decline, if the victims at least had their property returned.

This was not just a "case." It was a life event in which negotiation skills proved the only avenue to the achievement of the objective. Life is filled with such events. Therefore, the skills reviewed in this book are useful to everyone in almost every interpersonal interaction.

Choices are not easy. Neither is the determination of the goal and designing a strategy to meet it. Yet, when the goals are determined, choices are much easier to make.

The purpose of this book is to assist you in discovering the value of accommodation. Indeed, to win through accommodation means to win for the long haul. It also means giving up motives which may conflict with accommodation, such as retaliation and "winning" at all cost. The book details the use and practice of negotiation and mediation. Significant attention is devoted to a discussion of the sources of conflict and mechanisms and strategies for managing it. Questions of choice and ethics are discussed. The reader is guided through actual mediation sessions which demonstrate the techniques of reaching settlement in interpersonal conflict.

Accommodation is most easily reached through the assistance of a mediator; a neutral third-party, who negotiates on behalf of a settlement acceptable to both parties. Considerable attention is devoted to a review of the processes and techniques that produce settlement through mediation.

Unfortunately, there are occasions when mediators are not immediately available; when you must negotiate to achieve your own interest. Here, you must use the same techniques used by the mediator, in a much more difficult environment. Negotiating on your own behalf, is much less likely to achieve your goals than is mediation. Nevertheless, it is often the only practical way to solve the problem within the time available. Study mediation as a forum within which negotiation occurs. See the mediator as yourself. The degree to which you can approximate the skills of the mediator in those disputes which cannot be referred to mediation, the more likely you are to succeed.

Who should read this book? This book is intended for use by negotiators (and who isn't), mediators, both professional and role defined (such as mothers and teachers), managers who must motivate people to make profits, lawyers (who will settle most of their conflicts through mediation within the decade) and all students of human behavior who want to win and to find out what winning really means.

I. What Is Winning through Accommodation?

Winning is defined by the players in the game. If you "win" at poker, that may mean that you did not lose that evening. If you win a political race, that may mean that you got the number of votes necessary to assume the office, or it may mean that you made a case for your position, that you won a moral victory. For some people, winning can only mean that they got everything they wanted. For others, winning may mean that they prevented their opponent from getting what he wanted. Winning is a complex, multidimensional term with as many meanings as there are winners and losers.

The winning which is the focus of this book is the victory that can emerge when two contending parties succeed in getting what they *need,* while not necessarily getting what they *want.* This kind of winning is called accommodation. It involves understanding the needs of the other side and realizing that unless those needs are met, the argument will continue and that perpetuating arguments means losing.

Conflicts can be "settled" in one of four places. Many conflicts are probably "settled," which in this instance means perpetuated, in the streets through retaliation. Last year, 25,000 people were murdered in the United States. In at least 42% of these cases, the motive was unresolved civil disputes, often involving love or money. (Federal Bureau of Investigation, Uniform Crime Reports: September 20, 1980).

Another favorite forum for resolving conflicts has been the courts, which saw the processing of over 14.5 million lawsuits during 1982. (U.S. News and World Report, November 1, 1982)

Most of these lawsuits cost considerably more to process than the amount of money at issue.

A third method of conflict settlement is reserved for saints and people mentally healthy enough to forgive their opponents. This form of settlement, forgiveness or reconciliation, is fairly rare and requires that the conflict find settlement in the mind of each party.

The final option, resting somewhere between the courts and sainthood, requires bringing the issue to the table for discussion. Settlement outside the court and off the streets is called "alternative dispute resolution" by the American Bar Association. The term is probably not accurate, as we shall see, but it is certainly an improvement over the first term used by the ABA to describe mediation and negotiation. When such terms began to gain popularity during the late 1970s, the ABA established a committee on the "resolution of minor disputes." Their definition suggested that if only a little money was involved (little money for the clients or the attorneys?), the matter was a minor dispute. In any case, the current assumption is that mediation and negotiation are alternative forums for dispute resolution.

The very term "alternate" presupposes the existence of a predominant form of dispute resolution. That predominant forum for resolving disputes is presumed to be the legal system with its appropriate courts. Actually, there is little evidence to support the notion that most disputes are resolved through the courts. Indeed, there is considerable evidence to suggest that the predominant form of conflict resolution is negotiation, not litigation. This forum seems to find considerable use in criminal and civil matters and seems to be used in direct proportion to the amount of everything

1

at issue. The higher the stakes, the more likely negotiation or mediation will be used as processes of resolution. How often is one charge plea-bargained to a lesser charge in return for a guilty plea, even in murder cases? How often are international conflicts, which involve millions of lives and billions of dollars, mediated to settlement? The higher the stakes, the more ambiguous the issues, the more the parties finally incline to settle "out of court." Two disparate, but telling examples are the negotiations to release the American hostages in Iran and the negotiations relating to the IBM and AT&T anti-trust actions. Both issues were too "hot" and too complex to be settled through the court process.

What are these alternative processes of settlement? Essentially, there are only two alternatives. These types are distinguished by the nature of the settlement, which is either consensus based, or judgment based. Consensus processes require that the parties arrive at resolution without the imposition of judgment by an authority outside the dispute. Judgment processes permit the application of standards by an outside authority. This authority may be appointed by the parties, as in arbitration, or he may be appointed by the state, as in adjudication.

Consensus Based Alternatives

The principle form of consensus based alternatives is mediation. Mediation may be defined as the intervention of a neutral third party who, intervening at the request of the parties, assists the parties to find a resolution that fills their needs. The process of mediation demands that the mediator undertake three tasks. First, he must take control of the argument. Second, he must establish the negotiating distances between the parties. Third, he must generate alternatives from which the parties must select their own resolution. These tasks are thoroughly discussed in Chapter Four.

Negotiation is the second form of consensus based alternatives. When properly described and executed, negotiation demands consensus between the parties and insists in establishing equity in every settlement. In this light, negotiation may be defined as an attempt to achieve needs and some wants, while achieving an acceptable mixture of needs and wants for either party. Properly understood, therefore, the goals of negotiation and of mediation are exactly the same; construction of an equitable settlement based in consensus.

The pioneering Gerard I. Nierenberg has suggested that negotiation is the use of intense communication to satisfy divergent needs by expanding possible solutions. The similarity to the definition and function of mediation is astounding. Indeed, works by Roger Fisher, Thomas Schelling, Herbert Kelman and many others suggest that while one-sided agreements can only produce temporary winning, viable agreements and long-term winning require equity based in consensus.

It should be obvious that the principal difference in consensus negotiation and mediation is the presence of a neutral third party whose role is the creation of consensus. This difference is remarkably important. Without the third party neutral, there is no intervener. The self-interested parties are left alone, somewhat like two scorpions in a jar.

While it is possible to discuss, with considerable nuance, other titles for negotiation and mediation, these subtleties are of little more than academic interest. Conciliation, a process in which the parties are made ready for negotiation by reducing tension to a level which permits creative review, is one exception. However, conciliation is an on-going function within the mediation session itself, and rarely occurs as a singular event. Other processes, such as good offices or shuttle diplomacy, actually fit into the definitions of mediation or negotiation.

Judgment Based Alternatives

The principal form of judgment based alternatives is called arbitration. Arbitration may be defined as the intervention of a neutral third party who intervenes at the request of the parties, and who is empowered by the parties with full right, power and authority, to make a binding decision on the matters of controversy. Such a decision is called an award. The grounds for overturning such an award in a competent court are narrow indeed. An excellent source book on arbitration is *How Arbitration Works,* by Frank and Edna Asper Elkouri, Bureau of National Affairs, Inc., 1979. Generally, incompetency of the arbitrator, exceeding the authority granted the arbitrator or obvious bias are grounds for overturning the award. Each of these is very difficult to prove and very few awards are overturned.

Nuances also exist within the area of arbitration. For example, an infelicitous term called "med-arb" describes a process in which mediation proceeds until a few items remain at dispute. These remaining controversies are then submitted to arbitration. Another term cites a "mini-trial" approach to settlement, which often uses retired judges in expedited proceedings which occur in the twilight between arbitration and the more formal court processes. Again, each of these processes is distinguished by its premise which delivers to another the right and authority to decide matters at dispute between the parties. Other terms such as non-binding arbitration and advisory arbitration render decisions even though the disputing parties have not agreed to accept the decisions.

Another non-consensus based alternative is the more common definition of negotiation. Here, negotiation means "get all you can." Minimize your losses and maximize your gains. Full speed ahead and damn the torpedoes! This form of negotiation is really an attempt to intimidate the opposite, usually with threats of a deterrent or compellent nature. It is included here as a non-consensus based alternative because it begins with a judgment of rectitude and seeks to apply that judgment to the controversy. Unfortunately, the opposition quite often sees this as a declaration of war and resists with equal adamancy that which is advocated by the intimidator-negotiator. Most often, the result is either temporary victory or immediate, high-stakes loss.

While litigation is not considered to be an alternative process of dispute resolution, it is important to distinguish it by definition from the other processes. Here, a judge, appointed by the civil authority or the electorate is empowered with the authority to interpret and apply the "law" upon matters brought to his attention. The law takes no cognizance of emotion, rather it states the standard against which the behavior of the litigants is to be judged. It is the most powerful of judgment processes, and does not admit to the process of negotiation. It is fascinating to note, however, that without negotiation, the dockets would not be set and rearranged, nor would many of the lawsuits reach conclusion. The increasing use of masters' and judges' chambers is acknowledgment that the systems of judgment are often too slow and cumbersome to suit either the judges or the litigants.

Mediation

Since mediation is the principal forum within which consensus based negotiation processes occur, it will consume the majority of our attention in this book. It is useful to begin with a short history of mediation and how it came into current use.

Mediation was probably invented after negotiation, and in response to the frustration which accompanies adamancy based on a misunderstanding of what winning means. Nowhere was the ephemerality of "victory" more readily demonstrated than in the Italian City-States of the 14th and 15th centuries. Shifting alliances and mercenary armies made a friend an enemy and an enemy a friend again at every new dawn. The trust level was low. A neutral third party whom everyone would trust was desperately needed to minimize the loss of resources that accompanies every battle. The Papacy was instrumental in developing a foreign service with a real capacity to mediate conflicts. A common religion and spiritual fidelity to the Church's temporal leader was often sufficient to get the parties to sit down and discuss their differences. Communication, when well directed, can be most productive in limiting the extent of conflict if not always in preventing it. The early experience in international affairs contributed to the development of both mediative and negotiation arts. Note that Niccolo Machiavelli, who has been described as the father of negotiation, died in 1527.

Mediation was used more and more frequently throughout the centuries. Indeed, the establishment of Switzerland as a neutral state added a secular mediator to the list which had formerly included the Papacy and other religious authorities. National self-interest produced many mediative forums in the succeeding centuries, including cross-national problem-solving organs such as the Rhine and Danubian River Commissions.

The modern push for mediation began with the League of Nations and extended into the latter 20th century with the United Nations and its multitudinous commissions and special envoys. The European Economic Community and other such regional economic and political forums, all developed certain processes of internal dispute resolution.

On the industrial front, mediation was assisted in its development by the creation of the Federal Mediation and Conciliation Service, which has functioned under one title and authority or another since 1947. Without the Federal Mediation and Conciliation Service and the extraordinary ability of its mediators, the United States could have plunged into a period of economic chaos. It is amazing to realize that this tiny federal agency is the primary bulwark protecting the economy against unrestrained conflict between labor and management.

The United States Department of Justice also began using mediation in the 1960's because of intense racial conflicts. For the first time, the government recognized that mediation could apply not only to industrial and international conflicts, but could apply to interpersonal conflicts as well. The Community Relations Service of the Department of Justice still exists, albeit with many fewer mediators than during the sixties.

With the urging of then Attorney General Griffin Bell, the Law Enforcement Assistance Administration funded three centers for interpersonal mediation in the mid 1970's. One center in Atlanta, one in Los Angeles and one in Kansas City were funded to provide mediation services in interpersonal conflicts. Each tested the water for differing referral sources. By 1983, over 200 centers offered mediation to thousands of clients throughout the United States, Canada, England and Australia.

What Mediation Is Not

Mediation has been defined and its history reviewed. It has been contrasted with negotiation and with non-consensus modes of resolution. Mediation is often confused, even by mediators, with many other forms of intervention. While there is considerable room for discussion regarding the processes and techniques used in mediation, it is necessary to exclude certain approaches from the process.

Mediation is not crisis intervention. Crisis intervention may be defined as the timely intrusion into the life of a person, who, because of unusual stress, cannot handle his life in the ways he normally manages. The crucial issue is stress and its effect on usual functioning. While all of us handle stress of varying magnitudes in our own acquired ways, stress of unusually high proportions may render any of us unable to cope as we normally do. At such times, dispute resolution requiring rational thinking and involvement is not possible. Attempts to continue mediation, negotiation or arbitration under such circumstances will be unsuccessful and potentially dangerous to all involved. Crisis level stress may not only render the victim unable to deal effectively with disputes or conflict, but may also give rise to maladaptive behavior. Such behavior, unabated, may lead to serious emotional deterioration and even physical crisis. Crisis recognition and crisis intervention in mediation are vital. Crisis intervention requires certain skills that go beyond the mediation session and will be addressed in another section of this book.

Mediation is not counseling or psychotherapy. Both are differentiated from crisis intervention in terms of time allowed and required to assist the sufferer. While psychotherapy may require several sessions with the therapist over a period of time, crisis intervention necessitates immediate and emergency assistance. Each is differentiated from mediation in that counseling and psychotherapy begin from a premise of what constitutes health and probe deeply into the motivations for behavior. Mediation does none of these things.

Finally, mediation is not the practice of law. It does not tell the disputing parties what to do or what is "right." The parties themselves decide these issues. When advice is given regarding what the law says and what rights someone has, the intervener is not practicing mediation. Indeed, he may be practicing law. Whether the mediator is practicing law with or without a license, such practice is completely inappropriate and unprofessional if it occurs during mediation.

II. Theories of Conflict Management

Conflict is second only to love as a topic of intense study and literary preoccupation. It has been called the nation's most resilient growth industry. The investments made to control it unquestionably constitute an enormous percentage of the gross national product of this country and most others. The contexts within which conflict occurs begin at the internal, psychological level and quickly extend to the interpersonal, interorganizational, and international arenas. Indeed, conflict and the need for its control may be the principal animus for the creation of most of our socio-political systems. The courts, both civil and criminal, the police, regulatory bodies, and international organizations, are the forums within which military and non-military armies of professionals spend their lives dedicated to the management and control of conflict.

Conflict is usually subjected to theories of causation which are tied to the context in which the conflict occurs, or to a particular historical period or personality type. Therefore, the insights and nostrums for controlling conflict are issue and context specific. Academic researchers and advocates of institutional change have usually produced the same results; well intentioned, but arcane and untried strategies for international, interpersonal and internal peace. Thousands of pages and life-times have been consumed in the quest to determine the causes and cures of conflict. Unfortunately, very little of that effort has been productive.

An intensive review of the literature on the causes of conflict produces a division of theorists across five modalities on which the character of conflict and its cure are based:

1. Conflict is inevitable or preventable.
2. Conflict requires management or control.
3. Conflict arises from within each person or is "caused" by environmental conditions.
4. Conflict is productive or disruptive.
5. Conflict as an event and in respect to its causes is not fully understandable and predictable, or it is fully understandable and predictable.

The definition of conflict adopted here suggests that it is inevitable, manageable, internal and subjective, mostly productive and not fully understandable or predictable. *Conflict can be defined as a particular interaction within or between parties which arises when the perceived or actual differences between the parties are seen as relevant to an existing or contemplated event.* The elements of definition themselves contain the keys to strategic management of conflict, that is, permit the management of conflict through the use of various strategies to produce a particular event. The elements of this definition deserve some careful attention, since the entire process of mediation discussed in this book is premised on these elements.

1. *Conflict is a particular interaction.* This differentiates conflict from hostility or other such emotions. Conflict is a discrete event which arises in the cognitive interaction between that which is wanted (or needed) and that set of events or responses which appears to thwart the desired result.

2. *Conflict arises.* It does not exist until a precipitating event, often a statement or action, indicates that the desired result is not shared or cannot be accomplished without unacceptable costs.

3. *Conflict first arises within each of the conflicting parties.* It is often a sudden discovery that the ideal event or condition is not consonant with the expectations of the other party or permissible in cost or consistency to the individual with the conflict.

4. *Conflict may be based in the perceived or actual differences between or within the parties.* Since communication between parties is never completely effective and since the same errors and tendencies to deception occur within each of the parties, conflict is often based in the perception of differences, not upon the actual differences between the parties. When the actual differences are enumerated and understood by the conflicting parties, the conflict enters the range of manageability.

5. *Conflict occurs when the perceived or actual differences are perceived to be relevant.* Much of that which begins as conflict is based upon a perception of relevancy of events or conditions that have little to do with the actual differences between the parties. My desire to avoid being cheated ever again may suggest that my previous experience is relevant to a new conflict. The perception of relevancy of my previous experience is not shared by someone who has not suffered that experience.

The character of conflict permits management. If management is defined as the movement of people (man) over time (age) in service of a particular idea (ment) then management must focus on conflict. Simple movement, through the constraints of time and in the service of goals, is an effective producer of conflict. It is not surprising, therefore, that much of what we know about the management of conflict has arisen from industrial relations and from the management of enterprise.

Unfortunately, defining conflict is insufficient for its management. We must know more of its character.

Common Characteristics of Conflict

1. *Goals are always uncertain and changing.* Frequently, the goals posited by parties in conflict are goals which they have accepted with little reflection. Indeed, these goals are often the goals which significant others in their lives have suggested to them. A husband or wife, boy-friend or girl-friend might suggest: "Go for the limit. I wouldn't accept a penny less than. . . . Don't let them push you around." Confronting the arguments of the opposition and listening to the quiet, internal voice of logic and value may soften rigid demands. Unfortunately, it becomes difficult to explain to others why we "retreated," "chickened-out," or gave up our position. The internal prioritization of the goals is often quite confused. If one could choose between a Mercedes Benz and a Ford, the choice might be clear. If, however, one must choose between giving up a particular demand or generating unbridled anger in the other party, the choice is much more difficult. Thus, goals are not only uncertain, but they are and must be subject to change.

2. *Actors are always involved.* It is distressing that stating the obvious is necessary. We may all declare it obvious that people are actors in all disputes. Unfortunately, a common supposition dehumanizes the opposition by stating, "I'm having a fight with the bank," or, "I'm going to get even with my company for cheating me." Such depersonalization extends to the substitution of role for person. I may be having an argument with my "wife" or "neighbor," rather than with

Glenda or Ralph. The selection of referent to role is the first step in a long process of depersonalization that attempts to disguise the fact that all actors, all opponents, all negotiators, all attorneys, are really people, whom we label as representatives of institutions. This tendency is repeated, with potentially devastating results, when we defend against the Soviet Union or another enemy depersonalized into a country.

3. *Communication is always imperfect.* It is quite miraculous that any information arrives as intended. Communication is distorted by intention, inadvertence, distraction, environmental interference, physiological capacities, intellectual capacity, personal history, nuance, time pressure and level of complexity, to name but a few distorting influences. "I told you to do such and such," or, "I told you I would respond in such and such a way," produces only the illusion that the receiver has understood and accepted our message. Yet, much of our reaction as parents is based on the first command and much of our defense system is based on the second warning. Such assumptions that messages have been sent and understood are ludicrous at best and potentially lethal at worst.

4. *Values are always involved.* Regardless of pretence to the contrary, most human behavior is motivated by the search for achievement of some value. Rarely is behavior dictated by objective evaluations of outside parties such as judges, arbitrators, or other decision makers. Even when objectivity itself is declared to be the preeminent value, value continues to rule its own kingdom of subjectivity. More than one settlement has foundered on the rocks of "principle" as the conflicting parties see it. "It is the principle of the thing" often becomes the rallying cry of drowning captains and impoverished litigants. Even when the arbitrators of objectivity (the courts) rule, the ruling is infrequently obeyed until the issue of personal value has been sorted out by the parties. Values are always involved, but frequently only partially understood by their advocates.

5. *Feelings are always involved.* Most would agree that feelings are involved. Yet, most of the formal methods of dispute resolution, especially the court system, are designed to apply objective standards of judgment upon individual disputes without addressing the feeling of the conflicting parties. Part of the American elan requires suffering parties to "grin and bear it," even "keep a stiff upper lip," as do the British. Feelings are not only involved, but unless they are addressed sufficiently, the conflict continues with or without court process. The presence of feelings will often actively sabotage the agreements between the parties. Court orders stand empty and promises unfulfilled without an accommodation of feeling. One of the most frequently observed feelings in conflict settings is the fear of loss. It is often supposed that only a limited amount of money or good exists in any particular relationship. One or both of the parties assumes that unless he gets what is coming to him quickly, he may lose the opportunity forever. A frequent and important task of the conflict manager is to assist the parties in assessing the utility and accuracy of fear.

6. *Threats are always involved.* Most early socialization patterns in the United States and other Western countries emphasize the utility and propriety of deterrence theories in dealing with conflict. Therefore, preventing a particular action by threat of retaliation is the first "line of defense" adopted in interpersonal conflict. Deterrence is based on threats of action against the offending party. Deterrence acts as a basic premise of our system of fines, jails and police functions. It is also firmly entrenched in the traditional patterns of parent-child discipline. A similar tactic, compellence, seeks to compel individual action through the exercise of promises of action, rather than restrain it. This tactic is more frequently used in parent-child discipline than deterrence, but it also finds its way into our interpersonal behavior as "moral standards" which compel certain

actions. Again, implied threat is frequently the basis for compellence, albeit, compellence can find a basis in positive reinforcement. In any case, threat as a means of preventing "undesirable" behavior or in precipitating "desired" behavior is established in tradition, institutions and personality development.

7. *Money or some other material prize is usually involved as a cause for action, a cure for it or as a symbol of settlement.* The importance of material symbols of settlement does not reduce the respective importance of values and feelings. Rather, it reinforces their importance. Money itself is often viewed as the ultimate objectification of value; invested with the most intense of feelings. Money or some other material quantity often has an agreed common value, thus avoiding the ambiguous and relative values attached to such things as a handshake or apology. In industrial societies, money has a wide appeal. Therefore, money is frequently a topic of discussion and an element of settlement. Exceptions do occur. Parties may declare that the exchange of "mere money" might sully an otherwise principled exchange. This expression is frequently a tactic to avoid dealing with commonly acceptable symbols of value and should be carefully reviewed with the parties. Obversely, money can become an obsessive symbol of settlement precisely because one party perceives the other as lacking enough of it to bring the conflict to settlement. This tactic, often expressing itself in unrealistic "demands" is either sabotage or a failure on the part of the mediator in generating acceptable terms of settlement which are realizable by the parties. The role of money in any settlement demands careful review by the mediator and by the parties. What is the respective value attached to money in a particular settlement? Do the parties have the actual capacity to perform under the terms of the monetary settlement? What role is money playing within the settlement? The answers to such questions assist the mediator in constructing a viable settlement.

8. *Time is always an element in any conflict.* Since every element within a dispute is inexorably affected by the passage of time, time itself is an important element in every dispute. As a general rule, the longer the conflict continues, the higher the cost of ultimate settlement. The longer the dispute continues, the more adamant the feelings of the parties to the dispute. The notion that time heals all is not generally accurate. Individual histories seem to parallel those of Germany and Russia between the two great wars: "wait for an opportunity to even the score." Mortality and physical distance between combatants often encourages displacement of hostility on future or proximate parties, however. Additionally, the favorite phrase of contracts, "time being of the essence in this agreement . . ." takes on an added dimension, given the intensity of personal involvement in settlement. Shakespeare can be paraphrased to suggest that there is a tide in the affairs of disputes which when taken at its flood leads on to settlement; omitted, all of life itself may lie in despair. Finally, time itself has a subjective quality known only to the parties. Unless there is an attempt to objectify the meaning of time, the agreement is difficult to resolve and impossible to find performance. If one party declares that payment by the 15th of the month is acceptable and the other assumes the payment is late at one minute past midnight on the fifteenth of the month, the agreement may fail.

9. *Some commonly agreed upon facts always exist.* The neophyte negotiator and mediator is often confronted by a wall of conflict that appears unresolvable. Almost all paths of resolution may appear closed. Yet, the parties undoubtedly have some form of previous relationship that was

based in some common perception of facts. What are the commonly agreed upon facts? By fractionating the conflict, one defines the elements of disagreement. But unless the elements of common perception are identified, the agreement can not be reconstructed. For example, the subcontractor and the contractor to a business dispute may not agree upon the quality of a performance, but they may be able to agree that a specified number of beams or piers were to be installed. The aggregation of all points of agreement gives stark contrast to the elements in which disagreement still exists.

10. *There is always a desire to settle the conflict.* One can safely assume that if the parties are willing to discuss the dispute, there is some desire to settle it. Most often, at least one party to the dispute will begin by suggesting that either no dispute exists or by denying the necessity of settlement. The technician of conflict settlement will probe the reasons for each assumption, requiring each party to estimate the cost of continuing the dispute and of ignoring the perception of the other that a dispute exists. Frequently, the desire to settle is far greater than they consciously realize. If all efforts at "joint costing" have failed, the mediator should examine the benefits of maintaining the conflict for the parties. In domestic relations conflicts, for example, one party may assume that an argumentative relationship is preferable to no relationship at all. In cases of mental or emotional incapacity, one party may be truly unable to see the dispute with sufficient clarity to affirm its existence. These instances are rare. Among the sane and goal-oriented, the time and cost of settlement are always issues, but rarely is the eventual desirability of settlement at issue.

11. *Everything is negotiable.* Readers familiar with Abraham Maslow's hierarchy of needs may remember the order of homeostatic needs, safety and security needs, love and belonging needs, self-esteem needs, self-actualization needs, the needs to know and understand, and aesthetic needs. These are fascinating and thought-provoking categories. They are well discussed by G. I. Nierenberg in *Fundamentals of Negotiating.* Nevertheless, it should be noted that thousands of examples from daily experience offer evidence of people negotiating away even their own survival in service of certain "higher" ends, such as the survival of a loved one. When parties threaten to kill their opponent or deprive him of any of his other needs, the exchange of threats has begun. The response itself has set the parameters within which negotiation will occur. In disputes where one party refuses to communicate with the other, a form of negotiation continues. Such negotiations might be viewed as a tactical stage in which the parties are each attempting to "outlast" the other. In such circumstances, negotiation continues, but it does so with minimal communication and attempt at consensus. Such deadlocks are the ports of entry for many negotiators and mediators. Even during the session when one side suggests that his position is "non-negotiable," negotiation is continuing. Here, the responding party may suggest that given the non-negotiability of one factor to the dispute, he will make another, reciprocal factor non-negotiable. Are both parties willing to pay the costs of excluding certain issues from negotiation? If they express such positions, they are involving themselves in negotiation. Finally, since every position has a price and since at some level all prices are too high, the parties must negotiate. Ashleigh Brilliant, a cartoonist and the creator of "Pot Shots," has authored a cartoon in which one party suggests that he will listen "to your non-negotiable demands if you listen to my unacceptable alternatives." Such is the humorous proof that all things are eventually the topic of negotiation.

12. *All conflicts are eventually resolved.* Conflict between parties can be resolved internally or externally. If resolved internally, a psychological consensus or settlement is produced. Sometimes this settlement is called forgiveness. On other occasions, such settlements use the processes of cognitive dissonance to restructure thinking to resolve the strain between the desired behavior and the perception of actual behavior.

If conflict is resolved externally, it may find resolution in the courtroom as do approximately 14.5 million lawsuits each year. It may find resolution in the streets through retaliation, as additional millions do each year. Some disputes are resolved through attempts at avoidance. Such attempts often provide the illusion that the conflict has been resolved. The key to determining if the dispute has been resolved lies within the parties. Significant medical research suggests that problems avoided are not problems escaped. Stress, heart disease, ulcers and other maladies suggest that illness itself may be the agent of resolution by providing disputants with an early departure. Another possibility of resolution rests in finding an accommodation between the parties with which both the parties can live. All problems are eventually resolved. The parties themselves have the opportunity, sometimes, to select the method and influence the content of the resolution.

The previous discussion has summarized factors in conflict that seem to emerge frequently enough to be described as "common" to most conflicts. The emphasis here has been on the perceptions of the respective parties to any conflict. When conflicts do not find positive resolution, that failure usually arises from two sources: 1) the unwillingness of the parties to accurately, realistically and rationally examine the costs of continuing the conflict, or 2) the failure of the mediator to motivate the parties to examine the structure and assumptions implicit in their conflict and to identify and appraise the importance of their goals within the conflict. *Such lingering conflicts will usually exhibit the following characteristics:*

1. The goals of the parties have not been clearly established.
2. The costs of maintaining the conflict have not been clearly assessed by the parties.
3. The benefits of settlement have not been clearly articulated and weighed.
4. Each side is locked into the need to punish the opposing side.
5. One or both sides believes that another forum will resolve this dispute to his advantage.
6. One or both sides believes so firmly that his position is correct that he does not "need" to defend it or discuss settlement.

While failure to reach positive resolution is certain to occur, it can be avoided in most conflicts. Skill in conflict management accrues quickly when theory is combined and qualified by experience. These six dragons which maintain conflict can be slain in nearly every field of conflict. What strategies are currently employed in that battle?

Strategies of Managing, Controlling or Preventing Conflict

Strategies for addressing human conflict are defined by their respective approaches to the five modalities of conflict previously discussed. Four principal strategies for conflict management, control or prevention will be examined. While many variant strategies can be identified, each can be grouped in one of the following responses to conflict: Deterrence, Compellence, Avoidance or Accommodation.

Deterrence

The oldest, most frequently practiced and least effective strategy for dealing with conflict is deterrence. Deterrence can be defined as a method of conflict management which seeks to communicate that unacceptably painful consequences will attend the commission of proscribed actions. Deterrence is the very cornerstone of the military strategies of the U.S. and the U.S.S.R.

It is also the operating premise of our criminal justice system and a significant element in our system of resolving civil disputes. It is not accidental that it constitutes the systems of punishment popularly understood by the advocates of most major religions.

Deterrence assumes that conflict is inevitable, and that prevention and control is a form of management. Fortunately, this premise is no longer operative in our industrial sector (as it was during the early periods of unionization of the Ford assembly lines). It further assumes that while conflict might arise from internal sources, only external behavior need be controlled. Conflict is not viewed as potentially productive, and in fact, often is cast in life or death terms. Oddly, it assumes that the "offending" parties are rational and that their behavior is subject to modification, while simultaneously declaring that criminals and international enemies are not quite sane or such a system of potential punishments would not be necessary.

Deterrence exhibits other characteristics that demonstrate its ineffectivness as a productive management strategy. First, it is primarily past oriented. That is, deterrence only works as a preventive because it threatens to punish an action that has already occurred. While the supporters of deterrence in international relations suggest that it has "kept the peace," the penologists find little evidence that the death penalty or the promise of prison have a deterrent effect. Second, deterrence assumes that particular goals and standards of rectitude are definable, immutable and continuous. In doing so, it permits little latitude for negotiation. Third, because it is a retributory strategy, deterrence does nothing to change the premises of behavior, it only seeks to prevent the unwanted behavior from occurring. Finally, deterrence is personalistic, acting against the whole person, not against the behavior that is prohibited. It fails to separate the act from the actor.

Deterrence has a popularity that extends beyond the military, organized religion, the courts and the police. Assuming that the pervasiveness of its use establishes effectiveness, the general population buys guns, makes threats and promises punishment of their children as useful strategies for conflict control. It is as ineffective in interpersonal relations as it is on other levels of interaction. The successful mediator will assist the parties at dispute in re-examining the necessity of deterrence as a method of conflict management.

Compellence

Compellence is another strategy of conflict management that rivals deterrence in popularity and presumption of efficacy. Compellence may be defined as an attempt to compel an action or set of actions which otherwise would not have been done through the use of coercive force or reward. Attempting to compel someone to do a specific action is infinitely more difficult than preventing them from doing an action, however.

Compellence is the cornerstone of the traditional family and finds frequent employment at the work-place. In the family, compellence stands behind parental commands to do certain tasks. "Clean your room." "Come home by ten o'clock." In the workplace it finds uses which often approximate those of the home. "You will come to work by eight o'clock sharp." "You must do as you are told or as the contract says." It has the nature and assumption of commands.

Commands are based upon the presumption of authority, unquestioning obedience and a superordinate-subordinate relationship between the parties. It is not accidental that this strategy emerged from the traditional hierarchy of the family and continues to find safe haven in systems which require authoritarian decision-making, such as the military and fixed-rate assembly line manufacturing.

Compellence assumes that conflict can be prevented by the imposition of authority. It further assumes that when conflict does arise, it can be controlled. Conflict appears as an aberration caused by a temporary lapse of discipline or by external influences. Therefore, conflict is fully understandable and preventable.

Compellence shares substantial similarities with deterrence in its analytical assumptions, but has at least one major difference. Compellence is future oriented, since it demands future performance and expects the continuation of a predictable pattern of future performances. While deterrence can only punish actions which have already occurred, compellence posits future behavior. Compellence does assume, like deterrence, that there exists a particular standard of rectitude that is definable, immutable and continuous. Therefore, its operation proceeds from a deductive application of rules. It seeks to direct specific behavior and attempts to avoid acting against the entire personality. Unfortunately, like deterrence, it assumes that the determinants of behavior are external, not internally motivated.

The application of compellent strategies poses severe difficulties for its practitioners if the objects of its application do not behave. It can easily slip into deterrence strategy through the back door by declaring that "If you don't do as I say, the consequences will be painful." Such declarations usually draw perfunctory performance at best and may draw unexpected retaliation. If compellence is linked to a "positive" reward system, then it may promise future benefits for the worker, son, daughter or penitent. The difficulty here is that the behavior of the individual is dependent upon a constant repetition of reward. The agency offering rewards is confounded by the facts that rewards are not equally valued, rewards may decline in value through repetition and that the agency itself may run out of rewards in attempting to control behavior. In any one of these instances, non-conforming behavior may emerge and suggest that it is time to return to the punishment model to gain adherence to the expected behavior.

Examples of the failure of compellent strategy abound. Parents do not face an easy task when demanding certain actions on the basis of their presumed authority. "Do as I say, because I am your father," may arouse a resounding "No!" Now what? "If you don't behave in my house you can leave." "O.K., I'll leave." The score in this conflict is Parent—0, Child—0. The compellent reward system may lead to the same dead end. "If you do your chores and obey me, you will receive your allowance." "How much will you pay me to obey, today? Tomorrow?" It is odd that this same mechanism is used in industry. "Do your job, and we will pay you." "How much will you pay me to do my job today? Tomorrow?"

Compellent systems do not work for very long, since their internal rigidity prohibits them from changing tactics. Further, the costs of reward and the temptation to slide into deterrence models are ultimately overwhelming. The compellent model finds references in the courts when they declare: "Defendant is ordered to pay plaintiff the sum of $5000 within 30 days." Often, as is well evidenced by the number of empty judgments, the defendant will say "no" in a multitude of different ways, as can children and workers. They may say "no" by leaving the jurisdiction of the court or by declaring bankruptcy or by hiding assets or by retaliation. "Do it because I say so" does not make it as a strategy.

Avoidance

Avoidance may be defined as an attempt to avoid all decisions and actions required to find resolution to a conflict by pretending that there is no conflict and by allowing events to take their own course. Avoidance assumes that conflict is preventable by ignoring it. It presumes that conflict control arises from benign neglect. Here, conflict is supposed to arise from individuals, who are supposed to get tired, wear out and lie down. Conflict is definitely disruptive, so why entertain it? Conflict is predictable to the extent that it will eventually disappear without much effort.

Avoidance as a strategy is based on the assumption that if the shades are drawn and the doors locked, problems can be ignored. This strategy is the individualized equivalent of the isolationism that preceded the entry of the United States into the First World War. As such, it promises many of the same results: lack of preparation, unrealistic thinking, broken doors and torn shades. Its failure as a strategy for managing conflict is demonstrated by the rise in alcoholism, drug addiction, maladaptive behavior and crimes of retaliation in all societies.

Analytically, avoidant strategy is present-oriented. There is no future to worry about and the past is of no concern. It posits no standard from which to direct behavior, except the notion that problems can be ignored. It does act against the whole person, but the person it acts against is its user. It gives up all control, and hence all goal-directed behavior to the contending others in our lives by spending energy in the game of hide, ignore, and in so doing, prosper.

Since avoidance presumes to deny the efficacy of compellence and since, in avoiding any action, it denies the necessity of deterrence, it would appear to guarantee safety. Unfortunately, it not only requires constant effort, but encourages self-delusionary preoccupation. Few individuals can escape the interactions required of employment, relationship, transportation, housing and other day to day interchanges. During such interactions, interpersonal conflict is inevitable. To deny that the conflict exists requires increasing isolation and decreasing interaction. Most psychologists would not regard either tendency as healthy.

Behavioral manifestations of avoidant strategies are usually arrayed around the statement "I don't have a problem, he does." However, if the other party has a problem and you are somehow involved, *you* have a problem. The other party may try numerous efforts to draw the avoidant party's attention to the fact that a problem exists. Late night telephone calls, moth balls in the gas tank, poison pen letters, broken car aerials and the like are designed to obtain the attention of the avoidant party. When the avoidant party does not get the message and a particularly aggressive opponent is involved, the conflict usually escalates. Sometimes it escalates into murder. forty-two percent of the 25,000 murders reported by the FBI in 1982 were said to have arisen from unresolved civil disputes.

Nevertheless, avoidance is frequently practiced as a gambit with some promise of success. Of all the strategies discussed to this point, it is the most unpredictable in its immediate effects. Its long-term effects are more predictable, however. Even if the avoidant party does not have the misfortune to encounter a user of deterrent or compellent strategies, he must adopt a reclusive life style that is its own reward. Since such life styles are not fully compatible with life in complex societies, his choices are ultimately limited to change or withdrawal.

A more common variant on the avoidance strategy is the internalization of anger, frustration and feelings of injury. Here the conflict strategist does not choose to confront each individual problem with an individual agenda. Rather, he attempts to submerge the problem beneath his ordinary consciousness. This attempt usually finds the individual conflict displaced upon some other object of anger. If the object is not an inanimate object, then it is probably himself, a friend or lover.

Conflict, even if it is not recognized by the individual actors, goes somewhere. Its destination and the forum for its resolution can be a matter of conscious choice.

Accommodation

Accommodation is the most difficult and least frequently utilized strategy for managing conflict. It may be defined as a strategy for conflict resolution which seeks to discover the needs of each disputing party and to construct a settlement of the controversy which, while addressing those needs, also rests in consensus and equity.

Accommodation sets an incredibly ambitious agenda. It seeks neither to demand certain behaviors, nor prohibit them. It seeks to defuse past resentments, create a schedule for performance in the present and to minimize the cost and difficulty of future conflicts between the same individuals. It seeks to localize the conflict to a specific set of issues and to differentiate between the actions and the actors themselves.

The analytic orientation of the strategy of accommodation is inductive. It rests not in a deductive application of preexisting rules, but in the mutual and consensual discovery of common values between the conflicting parties. It posits only that equity is the cornerstone of all enduring agreements. Equity may be defined differently by the parties, but has an essential quality, which is often described as fairness, symmetry, reciprocity or equality. This search for equity requires consensus between the parties that arises not from coercion but from consent, freely given.

Accommodation posits the inevitability of conflict, while recognizing that its costs can be minimized and its benefits maximized through the creation of dynamic agreements. Living agreements that provide mechanisms for frequent renegotiation are viewed as the only practical method of creating a *modus vivendi* between the parties: an agreement that they can live with. Obviously, then, accommodation posits the notion that conflict can be managed, but cannot be controlled by outside forces or by one superior force. It further assumes that conflict can arise either from the environment or from the individual, but that most often, the conflict arises from the individualized, subjective interpretation of events which have been accepted by the parties. The strategy itself seems to make no judgment of the desirability of conflict. It only posits its inevitability and, therefore, the need for finding systems of managing it. Finally, accommodation implicitly assumes that since conflict is individualized and subjective, it is understandable only on an individual, case by case, basis. Principles of resolution and tools for finding that resolution exist, however.

Not surprisingly, accommodation has found its most frequent application in the dangerous world of international relations. Indeed, the entire international legal order is based on both tacit and explicit declarations of accommodation between conflicting parties. International law itself is based on a commonly shared, but dynamic, sense of equity and similar treatment. In this world of international relations, goals, values and priorities are highly variable. Yet, the need for creating a *modus vivendi* between the parties is ever pressing. The discovery and rediscovery of ways to continue living together requires accommodation. Where nations cooperate, one finds accommodation strategies at work. Conversely, where they fight, one finds a preponderance of deterrence, compellence and avoidance strategies.

Accommodation is the principal strategy of resolution utilized by mediation. Mediation, indeed, is a forum in which that strategy is practiced.

Accommodation is a revolutionary strategy. Some might suggest that it is the basis for certain forms of anarchy, since it denies the preeminence of any one standard of settlement and advocates the selection of standards by the conflicting parties themselves. This self-selection denies the right of the state or other authority to impose a standard of resolution on the conflicting parties. It also asserts that the formal, juridical system of conflict resolution does not resolve disputes, since it ignores the emotional, attitudinal aspects of all conflicts.

The process of accommodation requires the active participation of the parties at dispute. Its nature affords the possibility of rapid decision-making through the intervention of a neutral third party. It requires consensus before settlement can be asserted. It addresses the emotional and substantive issues at dispute. If carefully conducted, attempts at accommodation do not vitiate the legal rights of any disputant.

The strategy of accommodation is the strategy of preference adopted by the authors of this book. It is certainly not the only strategy for solving disputes. Likewise, other strategies can, and occasionally must, be brought to bear on a particular dispute. However, for disputes to find productive resolution, that resolution must rest in accommodation between the combatants. Mediation provides an ideal forum in which those resolutions can be constructed.

Conclusion

The four major strategies for managing have been addressed. It will be obvious to the reader that three of the strategies are viewed as inefficient, often inappropriate and antiquated. The next chapter will explore ways in which accommodation strategies are employed in a mediation setting.

Additionally, this chapter has defined conflict, posited five modalities across which the nature of conflict can be assessed and upon which each strategy hangs its theory, and suggested twelve characteristics of conflict which seem supported by the experience of the authors.

The reader is requested to look for examples of each of these strategies in his daily experience and to assess the effectiveness of each strategy in each conflict.

III. Mediation and Society

Mediation and Society: The Evolution of an Idea

"Terror" and "force," when they predominate in the social order, divide people into two basic sorts: the hunter and the hunted. The hunter carries the power of coercion. Although the hunter may attempt to persuade the hunted at various points in the hunt,[1] the "persuasion" in this instance depends so heavily upon the presence of coercive power that to say "persuasion" stretches the meaning of the term beyond its definition. The hunter offers no contract. At best, the hunter seeks to dictate the terms of surrender, and does not engage in the *quid pro quo* of mutual obligation and exchange.

Some might argue[2] that in instances where terror and force predominate, a state of nature, not a social order, exists. In the state of nature, the power of the mighty positively determines rights and obligations. Let us assume for our purposes here that terror and force are not associated only with the state of nature but with society as well. After all, a prisoner in a concentration camp and a litigant seeking compensation from a giant corporation may both *feel* terrorized and coerced.

Ironically, effective utilization of force requires greater and greater levels of cooperation among the hunters. More cooperation is required since labor must be carefully divided and relations founded upon some measure of mutual trust. The hunter perceives the need to spend time not hunting his own kind, concentrating instead upon the targets of the hunt. The irony derives from the contrast between the need for an internal peaceful order and the use of force upon others. The hunter faces psychological dissonance as the struggle for greater efficiency in the use of terror and force continues.

Each action of the hunter relies upon the sorting of two highly contrasted philosophies. The temptation is either to apply the philosophy of cooperation to dealings with the hunted, or the philosophy of force to relationships within the hunting group. Both choices contradict the premises of the philosophy of terror. Applying cooperative attitudes to dealings with the opposition creates room for maneuvering. Yet, applying the philosophy of terror within the group creates the fear and immobility that the same tactic uncovers among the hunted. Co-workers who are threatened tend carefully to stay within the confines of the rule that has been forcefully imposed. Creativity and responsiveness to unusual circumstances is inhibited. Covertly, intimidated workers may seek conscious or unconscious sabotage of their own group's desires. An overt response may involve joining forces with the hunted. Some individuals, faced with a set of only unacceptable responses, may become listless or even suicidal. Intra-group coercion unleashes forces of group disintegration.

In instances of overt and covert resistance to the coercive order of the hunter, a central motivating factor is the pursuit of control over the means of intimidation. Like any source of coercive power, control over the means of intimidation is a source of contention, since the possessor then has the means to achieve personal as well as group ambitions. The continued existence of the power source invites continued struggle.

The energy required to maintain internal group control, and, conversely, the competition for the means to internal control is energy that cannot be directed against the hunted. The social order which makes power possible with the energy of consensus is robbed by internal dissension, causing a decrease in the ability to sustain the hunt. Put simply, the hunt cannot be conducted as effectively while the hunters are squabbling among themselves.

The management of the internal struggle for power cannot be accomplished without reconciling the premises of cooperation and those of terror. The chain of events culminating in the destruction of the social order of the hunter may be traced in part to the creation of concentrated power, and to the failure to maintain a balance between the need to cooperate and the need to control.

The Forces of Cooperation

To the extent that the philosophy of terror is self-destructive, the philosophy of cooperation appeals to the instinct of survival and the assurance of acceptable levels of social tension. Survival demands a modulation of tension levels to create trust, which relaxes tension and enhances smooth interactions.

Mutuality in the ownership of power, although it allows the concentration of power in a mechanism like the legal system, does not in theory allow for the concentration of *personal* power, i.e. the personal ownership of the means of coercion. Mutuality, deriving from the perceived need for survival of the social order at acceptable levels of stress, sets the foundation for contractual obligations.

Obligations, to be contractual, are freely entered into and serve to distribute (or share) power between parties to the contract. The needs for survival, appropriately limited levels of stress, and trust create contracts of obligation and expectation.

A contract expresses at minimum the details of the steps taken for mutual obligation and expectation by recording decisions regarding "who," "what," "when," "where," "how," "how much," and (possibly) "what if" (see "writing agreements"). Mutuality does not preclude the possibility of loss, even mutual loss. But even in instances of loss, the social contract that evokes the need for mutuality in the first place need not be affected. The social contract is an entity that is independent of but included in individuals' transactions. The independent relationship between outcome and agreed upon processes heightens stability while providing an outlet for tensions. The outlet for tensions is the body of law expressive of the social contract, which the parties tacitly or expressly confirm as the context of their transactions.

Entering into contracts does not, however, totally assure mutual understanding. Agreeing to refer to the body of law in which the contract was reached does not establish total trust, eliminate all unacceptable stresses nor all destructive competition. Indeed, the body of the law to which contract theory refers is based upon an ideological and economic competition for the determination of rights and obligations.

Ideological and economic competition for these determinations relies in part upon the philosophy of coercion. Three major facts support this claim. First, the legal system relies upon coercive power (i.e., the power to imprison, confiscate property, wages) to enforce its determinations. The "winners" and "losers" in a law suit are engaging in a "hunt" for victory in a "zero-sum" game, as are the hunted and the hunter. In this context, victory means the confirmation of rights for the victor and obligations for the loser. The hunt is for the maximum expression of total power.

Secondly, use of the legal system requires the marshalling of economic forces. Time and energy can be brought to bear upon the outcome independently of theoretical considerations. Money, time, energy and expertise affect the quality of the presentation of an argument and even the likelihood that a case will be heard. The legal system is not isolated from economic considerations, and anything outside of the scope of the legal system is up to the parties themselves to determine. Determinations are reached that reflect not only legal rights and obligations, but relative economic power.

Third, the body of law, which represents the social context of contractual obligations, is reliant upon not only legislation which seeks to prescribe or proscribe specific behavior, but also upon case law. Case law (or precedential law) expresses a tradition. Arguments based in precedent essentially say, "We've done it this way before in this sort of instance. Since this instance is similar to the instance decided at an earlier time, the court should rule as the court earlier ruled. Therefore, the court should rule in my client's favor." An argument based in tradition binds the parties to highly specialized, little publicized and obscure rules to govern personal behavior.

In these three basic ways, imprisonment, the use of economic power and the use of precedential law, the legal system bears strong resemblance to the philosophy of force, since power plays a pivotal role. The issue of "right" as a moral or legal standard is either diminished or preempted by the issue of power.

The Mediative Event

Using mediation to resolve disputes marks a significant change. Although reliant upon contract law, and although economic and other power issues have not been isolated from consideration, the voluntary nature and the accommodative aura mediation radiates combine to soften the edges of the competitive struggle. The low cost of the process serves to equalize economic power for the settlement process itself. The informality of the language and the relative unimportance of previous outcomes, combined with the confidentiality and the relatively non-threatening nature of the proceedings, provides a firm contrast with legalism.

Clarification of mutual obligation as perceived by the parties is a major goal of mediation. The agreement serves to set forth solutions to a previously existing set of problems and to guide future behavior. Conflicts typically present a set of definable outcomes over which the parties are squabbling. Any contractual obligations entered into serve to record the choices mutually selected. Selecting and recording choices mutually agreed to supply two basic elements of a contract: assent and consideration. Consideration is derived from the nature of the exchange between the parties as determined by the choice of defined outcomes. Assent is required by the nature of the process.

An agreement reached in mediation is potentially reviewable in a court of law, and is best termed an "agreement" until or unless the document is adjudged to fulfill all the relevant requirements of the legal definition of a "contract." For example, if the agreement reached in mediation is based upon a misrepresentation of facts, then it would not be considered a "contract." Of course, an agreement may or may not be totally voided in the event that one or more elements necessary for a "valid" contract is missing. Since any mediated agreement is potentially reviewable, the set of outcomes chosen by the parties exists, not in isolation from, but in the context of the legal system which surrounds it.

The concerns expressed about the legal systems apply to mediated settlements. The substantial control and example of the legal system mean that power standards, as distinguished from abstractly fair or just standards, play an important role in settlements. The terms of the settlement are subject to the interpretations of the "win-lose" philosophy of the courts. Further, anticipating how well they are likely to do in court, the parties bargain with the "bottom lines" formulated by their perception of the legal system.

The relative economic status of the parties is also a factor which may affect the outcome. People with the resources to do research hire legal or other technical assistance to prepare documents to enter as "evidence" in the mediation. Those who can afford to wait for a settlement as long as it is necessary, clearly are in a position of strength regardless of the legal or moral status of the position which they take. This position of strength is not legally recognized as coercive, yet such advantages may "force" a settlement that one party is not happy with, and would not be willing to accept under other circumstances. There is an element of coercion, since the discussion is not conducted with purely moral (or legal) considerations as the focus of decision. Power intrudes.

Not all agreements entered into in mediation or in any other circumstances can eliminate coercive factors. But eliminating the coercive element, however desirable that may be, is not necessary for a "meeting of the minds" to occur. In much of life, agreements are made and must be made even though people cannot come to an agreement that excludes coercive elements. Husbands and wives, parents and children, police officers and motorists, blacks and caucasians all benefit from living together peacefully. If everyone waited for the perfect accord, most of us would do nothing but wait. Waiting for the perfect accord may be like waiting for Godot: an endless debate about that which may never exist.

Agreements made in the presence of coercive factors like social and economic differences must therefore be allowable in mediation, except where the social-moral order has determined that certain agreements are unallowable. For example, a settlement in which someone "agrees" to be sexually harassed or discriminated against can be rejected as an allowable contractual exchange by the mediator's withdrawal. But one individual in a better economic position bargaining for a better outcome, in the present socio-legal context, is not prohibited from using such advantages. A fair conclusion is that, in the present context, mediation does not, cannot and should not be required to eliminate all the coercive elements from the settlement process.

Those who see mediation as a panacea for all social disaffections may not be pleased by this statement. Yet there are good reasons to be enthusiastic about the growing importance of mediation. Despite the fact that mediation is not a cure-all, its inclusion in the dispute resolution process is a new, if still faint light of the dawn of a new age in conflict management.

The Accommodative Edge

A key element necessary to the control if not elimination of the coercive element is the volitional entrance into a consensual agreement. Ideally, one might wish for a positive motive for agreeing, rather than an avoidance. But having the opportuniy to enter into an agreement to avoid unpleasant consequences (like having to spend money for an attorney), as well as to obtain inherently desirable outcomes, is advantageous on its own terms. The advantages derive from the lower cost of the process of mediation, the opportunity to personally address the opponent, and the opportunity to resolve the vital issue of feelings.

Lower costs derive from numerous factors. First, many disputes are complicated by highly emotional issues. Since mediation is not predicated upon the determination of rights, the inclusion of which "raises the stakes" and distracts attention from settlement, emotionally significant issues can be addressed. Second, many disputes involve small sums of money. The involvement of volunteers in instances of this sort minimizes the need for high-cost legal professionals. The absence of the need to learn a highly-specialized vocabulary further reduces the need for professional involvement of "interpreters" to communicate the meaning of events to their clients.

Third, scheduling is uncomplicated by the need to coordinate the activities of large numbers of people. Litigation requires a clerk, a bailiff, the judge, perhaps a jury, the two attorneys (at a minimum), and the parties or their representatives, plus witnesses and months or years. In contrast, a mediation session requires only the parties and a mediator, plus outside advisors to the parties in more complex matters.

Fourth, because mediation is capable of dealing more effectively with the affective issues, the total time involvement of the parties is less than that experienced by litigants. This effectiveness derives from the sensitivity of mediation to the emotional needs of the parties. Where litigation has its nearly exclusive focus upon substantive and procedural issues in the paternal pursuit of the best interests of the parties, or in the deductive comparison of the situation to the relevant legal norms, mediation focuses more upon emotional needs. A mediator's job requires one to take time to listen to people unburden themselves. Allowing people to "vent" their emotions, and guiding them through the choices their own minds create, allows the discovery of a solution, which in many instances, is emotionally based. Dealing with the emotional and substantive issues as seen by the parties helps prevent the generation of new issues (by means of motives or discoveries) that are new to the parties but required by the legal process.

Purely financial issues or other less emotional problems can also be effectively managed in mediation by excluding legal concerns. Often individuals or businesses are concerned with their financial arrangements and not with the legal implications of their activities. The consumer may want a refund (not victory under the statutes of fraud) or a landlord may want furniture returned (not an indictment). When the amount of money is small or the potential seriousness of the problem limited, the impetus for legal involvement is minor. An extra-legal resolution is acceptable in light of the magnitude of the problems which are often faced.

Even in situations where people do not reach an accommodation in mediation, they are able to review their opponent's position and portray their own "reasonableness" to their opponent. In "feeling out" the other side, they may be able to evaluate their likelihood of success if they pursue other avenues.

Whether the parties' issues have low or high emotional content, the relatively low cost and high efficiency of mediation reduces the importance of discrepancies in power between the parties. The reduction is not only a consequence of cost efficiency, but also of the "win-win" philosophy mediation expresses. The legal atmosphere encourages not a "win-win" but a competitive "win-lose" approach to problem solving. Although mediation probably cannot eliminate destructive competition, neither is it encouraged.

The mediator returns frequently to the question, "How can everyone win?" This question jars the competitive pattern (encouraged by the adversary system) of the hunter and the hunted. The win-win philosophy is in complete contrast to the win-lose stance. The hunter seldom seeks to benefit the prey. But the mediators ask for the consideration of mutual benefit. The hunted only seeks to fight or flee, not to understand and accommodate the needs of the "hated foe." The mediator, in effect, tries to change the goal of the game from "zero sum" to "maximum sum."

A possible effect of this change is demonstrated in research conducted by Morton Deutsch.[3] Deutsch set up two games of chicken. In one, Deutsch instructed his subjects to proceed as close as possible to a point of no return. Beyond that point lay a formidable obstacle. The winner of this contest was the one that turned away from the obstacle at the latest moment (and who also, by the way, was the one most likely to head over the cliff or into a formidable obstacle). The outcomes were measured as a composite score. For example, if one party came within a measure of "2" and the other party to a measure of "1," the composite score was "3." The winner scored "1." In a variation of the game, Deutsch instructed participants to pre-arrange a signal such that both parties were to simultaneously veer from the obstacle at the latest safe moment. Outcomes were measured. The result was that greater overall scores were obtained in the variation when the parties turned away from the obstacle simultaneously.

This research is by no means conclusive. The desirability of total victory is a value that is difficult to measure in simple terms. The research does not demonstrate why (or if) increased total scores are more desirable. The research does not demonstrate that mutual trust is achievable as easily as it was in the research. No doubt there are methodological criticisms to make. Yet the study is useful. It indicates that a greater total score is more desirable than a lesser total score, and cooperative "win-win" strategies produce this result consistently.

One choice is between measuring outcomes on an individual basis or as a total of the social interactions. The former is desirable to those who believe that society is better off when strength emerges through win-lose competition. The total outcome is in the interest of those who believe that society is a collection of interactions which cannot be isolated from one another. Yet the contrast is between the philosophy of force (which can be called the "zero-sum" philosophy) and the philosophy of cooperation (the "maximum sum" philosophy).

While law is based upon the zero-sum game, mediation is based on the maximum sum solution. The distinction is not an absolute, but rather one of emphasis. Lawyers negotiate outcomes by representing their clients' best interests in winning. But the mediator is sensitive to both parties, and is naturally attracted to the maximum-sum outcome as mutually observed.

The modification of the influence of power occurs in mediation by means of the mediator's persistence in helping clients find ways of accommodating all or most needs. Lawyers can and do adopt this stance, but their position as an advocate does not reflect a commitment to accommodative outcomes. And the legal system often provides a powerful element in the bargaining process, often a coercive one. Further, because clients incur fees even if the case is settled by their attorneys prior to hearing, the role of economic power and other coercive considerations is enhanced.

Conclusion

Mediation contributes to the de-emphasis of coercive considerations by its lower cost and the pursuit of mutual needs. For example, a consumer benefits by not having to hire legal counsel and, despite a greater ability to retain counsel, businesses are interested in reducing costs. The mediator can draw forth the mutality of this need to encourage compromise or the creation of new solutions.

Thus, although mediation does not preclude power considerations, its use produces a more desirable outcome as measured mutually. The reduction of settlement costs is one specific example of the benefit of the mutual measurement of outcomes. The difference between mediation and the law, is the mediator's belief that the achievement of greater total benefits is more desirable than individualized outcome measurements.

In its simplest form, society is dominated by the struggle for power. The win-lose philosophy of the legal system, however, encourages a struggle for legal rights in a zero-sum game. Mediation does not exclude coercive considerations, but the "win-win" philosophy encourages the mutual measurement of the outcome and deemphasizes the role of coercive considerations. Mediation encourages the exchange of the hunter-hunted for equitable partners engaged in the quid pro quo of exchange.

Notes

1. Bettleheim, Bruno. *The Informed Heart.*
2. Hobbs, Thomas. *Leviathan;* ed. by C. B. Macpherson, Penguin Books, 1975.

IV. An Overview of the Process of Doing Conflict Management

The reader will recall that the mediator has three procedural tasks to perform in every mediation session. First, the mediator must take temporary control of the argument, thus creating a sense of security for his clients. Second, the mediator must establish the negotiating distances between the parties by differentiating needs from wants. Finally, the mediator must generate alternatives from which the parties can select the alternative perceived by them to be the most equitable. Additionally, the mediator must assist the parties in framing the agreement between them.

The three tasks of the mediator are accomplished by the use of direct questioning, caucusing, joint-costing and position restatement by each side in contention. Directed questioning seeks to set in motion processes of self-examination. Questions used here are value-free, but confrontive. For example, "What will it cost to continue this dispute?" sets in motion the process of self-examination. However, the question, "Don't you think the cost of continuing this dispute will be unacceptably high?" might be viewed as a parental conclusion. A series of such questions linked together with a common strategy unmasks the elements of conflict which often masquerade as points of substance, but are actually issues of feeling. When the masquerade is over, the parties probably will have discovered that what they want (desired results) and what they need (irreducible requirements) are very different quantities. They also will discover that many more alternative futures exist than those which they brought to the negotiating table. These techniques are more thoroughly discussed later in this chapter and in special sections of the book.

Taking Control of the Argument

Taking control of the argument is a complex and immediate task. The mediator must accomplish four tasks in this activity. First, the mediator must secure, to the best of his ability, the safety and security of the clients. Second, the mediator must establish rapport, confidence and trust with his clients. Third, the mediator must set the stage, detail the process agenda for discussion and introduce the concept of mediation and its search for accommodation. Finally, the mediator must maintain control of the process from the introduction to the articulation of the agreement.

The safety and security of the clients requires mediator planning. First, a background familiarity with the clients, their history and the issues at dispute must be accomplished. This may be done through a careful process of intake and interview. The goals here are to provide a general assessment of the sanity, capacity and proclivity of the clients. Clients with a tenuous grip on reality can not mediate or negotiate intelligently. Here, the obvious cases of mental incapacity can be referred to appropriate assistance. The client must possess sufficient intellectual capacity to discuss the issues and sufficient emotional stability to handle the stress that awaits him in the mediation session. Elements of personal history, such as habitual violence or possession of weapons, often will be dramatized by the responding party to the dispute. Such warnings must not be ignored. Weapons affidavits should be utilized, not as a means of preventing weapons with a piece of paper, but in requiring the parties to confront the possibility of violence. Finally, the issues at dispute must be assessed and the mediator prepared accordingly. The more intense, the longer the duration of the conflict and the more affective issues involved, the greater the likelihood of high emtoions. In such instances, the mediator may wish to consider caucusing with the parties in separate rooms or over the telephone before the mediation session is held.

Taking control of the argument is a volitional act on the part of the disputing parties and on the part of the mediator. Such control is exercised only during the mediation session and only for the purposes of assisting the parties in forging an agreement. If used for the ego gratification of the mediator or to move the agreement closer to the "ideal" solution favored by the mediator, the parties will rebel and the session fail. The mediator must also realize that when the parties conclude the session, the responsibility for controlling the dispute returns to them. In this context, one of the most powerful tools of settlement possessed by the mediator is the threat to withdraw from the mediation, leaving the parties in control of their own chaos again.

Establishing rapport, confidence and trust with the clients is a subtle business. The task begins with the first moment of contact, whether over the telephone or in person. The mediator must make rapid assessments of mood, humor, special sensitivities and relative power between the parties. Unfortunately, this process is largely intuitional and extremely difficult to describe in detail. Practice with simulations which involve different cases and widely divergent clients is the most effective manner of learning. Nevertheless, several general rules do apply.

First, the parties must be convinced that your interest in assisting them is both genuine and based in competency. For this reason, your introduction of yourself might include some background information on your experience and credentials in mediation. Secondly, the parties must be convinced that you are capable of acting as a neutral party and that you have no interest in the nature of the outcome. This can be conveyed by a simple statement that affirms that neither of the parties knows you and that your interest is in reaching a settlement based in consensus which does not require nor permit your approval or disapproval. Here, the mediator must state his ethical requirements for proceeding. One might say that ". . . my interest is in helping you reach an agreement based in consensus and equity." "I will not assist you in reaching just any agreement because you are tired or because one side has greater temporary power than the other." "I have ethical and moral concerns and will express them to you should they bear on this process in any way." Third, the parties must be convinced that you can not be cajoled, complimented or persuaded to buy either position. The clients will certainly test you on this point. "You tell me who is right!" "Isn't his argument stupid (or unfair)?" Such statements are attempts to win your favor which, if successful, will destroy the opportunity for successful mediation.

The process of establishing rapport in mediation is not the same process which you might find appropriate at a cocktail party, however. The formal "Mr.", "Ms." or "Mrs." are ideal means of maintaining a degree of formality that lead to rapport and control. The imposition of titles such as "Doctor" or "Councilman," may inadvertently assist the titled person in obtaining a superordinate position. This can lead to feelings of inferiority on the part of the opposite party. Ask permission of the parties to use any title before proceeding.

Setting the stage, explaining the process of mediation, and establishing the agenda are also necessary. Setting the stage, particularly as it relates to the configuration of the physical environment is so important that a section of this chapter has been devoted especially to it. It is sufficient to say that the seating arrangement has a dramatic influence on the sociometric patterns between the parties.

Explanation of the process of mediation can actually inspire the parties to keep a task orientation throughout the meeting and assist the mediator in maintaining control. The explanation should contain five elements. First, the definition of mediation must be offered in a way that is easily understood by the parties. Next, the parties must be asked to commit themselves to proceed diligently and to begin a reexamination of their favored solutions to the controversy. Third, the rules of the session must be articulated and commitment to those rules secured. These rules usually include: no interruptions, no rebuttals that are designed to attack the person, emphasis on the problem not upon the personalities of the parties and active participation by both parties. Fourth, the mediator must protect the integrity of the process by requiring the parties to waive their right to subpoena him and the documents produced in the discussion and to hold him and his agency harmless for the effect of any and all agreements that emerge from the process. This element is quite complex and requires careful planning and assistance from competent counsel to draft the necessary forms. Finally, the parties must be told that a specific time of adjournment may be desirable and that the mediator may meet with the parties privately in a caucus. These rules prevent fatigue from gaining a preemptive negotiating power and assure that the mediator may use the valuable tool of caucusing, if needed.

Establishing the agenda virtually controls the meeting. The mediator must, therefore, control the agenda. The agenda should be designed to secure the three goals of mediation. It should accomplish five tasks. First, it should reserve time for each side to articulate all of the general issues. Second, it should require each side to restate what they heard the opposite party say the issues are. Third, it should permit the mediator time to fractionate the issues. This is a term used by Roger Fisher of Harvard University. It simply reflects the fact that you can not effectively discuss all of the issues at once. Each issue must be identified as parts of a puzzle. After each issue has been examined, assessed and reviewed by each side, then, and only then, can it find its natural place in the settlement. Fourth, it should provide for the achievement and review of interim agreements. This means that tentative agreements can be constructed on part of the controversy during each session. Finally, it should provide for a commitment to return to the next session, if one is necessary, and establish the ground rules for behavior between the sessions.

Maintaining control of the mediation from the introduction to the construction of the agreement is essential. The mediator knows that control has been lost when an injury occurs, one or more of the parties leaves or when one party gains clear control of the agenda and the process. Maintaining control requires vigilance and intense concentration and careful listening. The maintenance of control requires the performance of four tasks. First, the parties must be kept on the agenda and prevented from sliding into long winded and self-indulgent reviews of their feelings. Second, the mediator must balance his need for control with the clients need to discuss the issues with one another during the session. If too much control is exercised, the parties may feel suppressed. Not enough control by the mediator can permit one client to gain control of the process. Third, the mediator must enforce the rules that have been established for the process; reminding the clients of their previous commitment to those rules. Finally, the mediator must listen to himself and monitor his own feelings regarding the conflict. The mediator must maintain confidence of the clients. That confidence rests on the clients' perceptions of the mediator as fair and competent. Maintaining fairness and competency requires careful self-monitoring.

Establishing the Negotiating Distances

The second task for the mediator brings him to the very edge of counseling and psychotherapy. Before the conflict can find resolution and the parties an accommodation, the needs and wants of each party must be identified, prioritized and compared. This task is especially difficult, since our national history and child-rearing practices seem to suggest that what you want is what you need and vice-versa. Most continuing arguments, whether regarding commercial transactions or domestic disputes, involve parties who have not sorted out what they need from what they want and the highest permissible cost of acquiring each.

The establishment of negotiating distances between the parties involves four steps: (1) defining needs, (2) defining wants, (3) establishing the distances between the needs and wants, and (4) securing commitments to proceed to the generation of approximate mixes of wants and needs for both parties.

Defining Needs

A need may be defined as an irreducible minimum requirement without which the organism would cease to function on a level acceptable to the organism. Note that functioning on an "acceptable" level can be easily confused with one's desires or wants and often is confused. For example, a need in our modern society might be the necessity for transportation. Either party might desire a Mercedez Benz automobile, but they need transportation.

Defining needs is an intensely psychological process that, while it occurs within the mind of the client, it is set in motion by the mediator or the negotiator. Needs are often defined within three levels of thinking; the functions of the needs, the structures of the needs, and the duration of the needs. It is beyond the scope of this book, and of mediation itself, to examine the structure of the needs and wants, for this structure is intrinsically bound up with the personality of the parties. This is the province of psychology. The duration of the needs is a function of awareness within each individual and might be described as the province of spirit or religion. The functions, however, can and must be addressed in mediation and negotiation.

The functions which the needs perform may be described as psychological, physiological and relational. Such needs are often described in terms set forth by Abraham Maslow in his hierarchy of needs. While this paradigm is useful, it can become quite complex and obscure. Therefore, it has not been employed here.

Psychological needs are the irreducible requirements upon which the psychological structure of the client is based. These needs differ widely within and among each individual, they also are subject to change over time. Psychological needs are often stated as the principal needs of the contending parties with phrases indicating that "it is the principle of the thing." The use of directed questioning will, if carefully executed, reveal the conscious psychological needs of the parties. These needs frequently include the need for maintenance of self-esteem, the need to be consonant with one's own value structure and the need to achieve a tolerable level of stress. The client can state these needs in the private caucus, without the pressures of the opposing party. With the information achieved regarding the psychological, often symbolic, needs of each party, the mediator can guide the discussion to address these needs. Mediator or negotiator must discover these needs and insure that they are addressed in the final settlement between the parties.

Physiological functions are usually much easier to determine and to demonstrate. For example, a divorcing couple with children knows that a certain level of financial support is necessary to sustain the children. The physiological needs of the children are demonstrable. Likewise, the parties themselves, know that a certain level of income is required to sustain their lives. Other physiological needs are not as obvious. The mediator knows that physiological needs intrude into every session. Clients can sustain a high level of conflict for only short periods of time. Intense anger, frustration and hostility must be dissipated or the organism will not function. The human physiology permits only brief periods of intense concentration. Likewise, wise negotiators will schedule sessions only after both parties have eaten and are prepared with sufficient energy to proceed. Obviously, the mediator or negotiator also has physiological needs which demand his attention. Ultimately, the parties realize that the only absolute, immediate physiological need is to maintain 98.6 degrees of body temperature.

Relational needs are often overlooked. Both parties have relational needs that may spring from their desire to maintain their relationship or a relationship with another party who will be affected by the outcome. For example, many negotiations have failed because the agent of settlement failed to discover that the positions taken by the parties had nothing to do with their ostensible needs. Rather, the attitude of an absent party, such as a father, spouse, boss or other influential peer had instructed the disputant regarding the appropriate position. The mediator or negotiator must discover the relational needs of the parties so that the agreement can address those needs in a manner capable of filling those needs.

Defining Wants

Every negotiation session bristles with the articulation of wants from each party. Further, wants are most often presented as irreducible needs. Unfortunately, wants are often inflated by each party in fear that the other party will attempt to negotiate most of them away in any case. Therefore, it may surprise the uninitiated that defining the wants of the parties is almost as difficult as discovering their needs. The parties may themselves be confused regarding what they want and what they have been told that they want.

Discovering the nature of the desires of each party involves the mediator in examination of the nature of the wants. As in the case of needs, wants can be described as psychological, and relational. Very few physiological wants can be discerned; most are needs.

Psychological wants ordinarily relate to the perceived internal distance between what the party views himself as being and what he would like to be. For example, if one party views himself as weak but he would like to be assertive, this desire may urge him to posit an unattainable goal, simply to prove his reach. His wants may assert the desire for a twelve room house, where he would live alone, because he would like to see himself as rich. Such wants are extremely powerful for they may be closely entwined with a perceived need to move toward an ideal circumstance. What are the psychological wants of the parties? Can they be addressed in the agreement?

Relational wants are the most difficult of all wants to address. Here, the opposing party may wish intensely that a certain relationship existed between himself and a former spouse or an employer or a neighbor. Again, the relational wants are identified as a statement of an ideal; different from what the relationship is.

Establishing Distance between Needs and Wants

After a conscientiously applied strategy for defining wants and needs, the distance between these two factors would seem to be clear. Indeed, the distances are often very clear. They may also appear to be beyond conciliation. Here, the mediator must assist the parties in discovering the costs of maintaining each distance. It is important here to stress that the mediator does not condemn the parties for the wide distances between their needs and their desires.

However, the primary incentive to settlement arises from the discovery that each need and each want has an inherent cost for attainment. How much is that cost and is it worth it to the "buyer?" The discovery of cost has already begun, because the skilled mediator or negotiator has assisted the parties in *defining* their needs and in *differentiating* what they want from what they need. It is extraordinary to find that some people may have never examined their ambitions in any disagreement beyond arriving at an immediate conclusion that they are "right."

The parties "own" their positions, including the conclusions they have reached regarding their wants and needs. Now, the mediator must discover their *objective in this dispute.* How would you like it to turn out and what are the costs of achieving that outcome? The costs range from the highest, which can be death or failure to agree, to the lowest which is agreement and accommodation. Like needs and wants, the objective in the dispute is usually a simplistic assertion that was arrived at with little thought, adopted and memorized. The greatest movement in most negotiations comes when the parties compare their needs and their carefully reexamined wants to the objective they came in with. A discovery of the true nature of their needs is often sufficient to begin a process of rethinking that changes the objective to an attainable goal. The mediator helps the parties achieve this through the use of questioning, well discussed in another chapter.

Securing Commitment to Proceed

The patient is now open and the problems clearly disclosed. The remaining essential question is this: "Does the patient want to survive?" You may surmise that this analogy is overdrawn. Yet, in many instances of interpersonal conflict, settlement itself is a matter of survival of the parties. The question now posed by the mediator is "Do the parties want to find an agreement?" The will to move from the comfortable and known terrain of a particular dispute to the new ground of resolution is a difficult decision. It is often easier to maintain the argument. But what is the pay off? What needs are being met by perpetuation of the dispute?

The mediator must secure a willingness to approach the agreement. Without this affirmation of intent, the parties may often sabotage the agreement at the last minute. In such instances the mediator may have failed to discover that one of the base needs of the parties was to continue the conflict.

If the parties are actively and clearly willing to proceed the mediator must set forth their homework. Three tasks must be performed in preparation for the agreement. First, the parties must agree to examine their well defined needs *in the light of the needs of the other party.* Both parties must find a way, a *modus vivendi* which will meet the needs of each. This can be accomplished through careful thought at some new surrounding, such as the public library or a Christian Science Reading Room. New surroundings will often avoid the subtle clues which reinforce the old positions. Next, each party should commit to generating new alternative solutions that have never been discussed before in the sessions. These alternatives will contain possible avenues of reconciliation. Finally, the mediator should commit to a period of intense thought to generate alternatives from which the disputing parties may select a viable future settlement.

Conclusion

The three tasts of the mediator have been defined. The complexity of these tasks can only be introduced in this short section. Each task merits your thought and your experience to bring it to life, adapt it to your own purposes and make it useful.

The final topic of "agreements" is a separate topic which deserves extensive treatment and receives it in another section.

The Setting in Mediation

The setting in which the mediation takes place is important for gaining and maintaining control of the argument, facilitating communication, reducing or increasing pressure on the parties, and assuring the safety of all those involved (see "Safety and Weapons"). These factors will be discussed in light of the effect of variables in the choice of room size and atmosphere and the size, the style and color of all furniture, and mediator attire.

Furniture

Table shapes have specific effects upon the mediation process. Tables are rectangular, square, multi-sided or round. They are of different heights and sizes. Rectangular tables have head and foot positions. The head position is distinguished from the foot by the relative status of who sits there. People may jockey for a particular spot, and those who occupy them have an advantage insofar as those positions command attention derived from tradition and the convergence of the lines of the table on the position (See Figure 1). Mediators who use rectangular tables should take one of the ends and discourage anyone else from sitting at the other end. This can be accomplished by removing the chair from that position and directing the parties to their seats, as is often done by a host or hostess at a dinner.

Figure 1

Rectangular tables have hard, square lines. Our experience indicates that they seem to encourage interchanges that parallel this feature. No formal study encountered confirms or denies this assertion, but until a more definitive evaluation is developed, rectangular tables should be avoided.

Square tables have four equal sides, which suggests an equality between the parties. There is no "head" position. The eyes are as easily attracted to one position as another. The matter of control, then, depends on other factors, such as non-verbal communiques, status, dress and the like. No party, including the mediator, can command a superior sitting position. This table shape is recommended over the rectangle.

The round table is the preferred shape (See Figure 2). In the legend of Arthur, the round table symbolized in part the equitable relationshhip of peers gathering together to solve the problems of injustice. The total lack of dividing lines, present even in a square, suggests the diminution of differences and maximizing of unity. From any point on the circle, the view of the center and all the other seats is the same.

The second major variable is size. Tables can be as small as three feet in diameter (See Figure 2) or 8 feet or longer. Smaller tables provide closer proximity, which can mean greater or lesser levels of tension, depending on sexual differences.[1] Smaller tables leave the parties more open to violence, as they are within more convenient striking distance. Larger tables may be safer, but they violate the perception of appropriate closeness between people.

A third major variable is height. Tables vary in height from about 18 inches (coffee-table height) to about 30 inches (desk top height). Smaller tables put fewer barriers between people, but make it more difficult to write and lessen safety. The decreased barriers may encourage conversation due to the informality of the setting. Desk-top height tables provide a more significant barrier, adding slightly to the perception of safety, and make writing easier.

Figure 2

The choice among table shapes should vary according to the type of case. More formal settings may be more comfortable to business operators, less comfortable to consumers, more conducive to resolving disputes in on-going close personal relationships, and most desirable in situations involving a high degree of danger where the setting should be used to accentuate the importance of abiding by the rules. Figure 3 portrays an informal, relaxed arrangement that seems to be working well.

In addition to the preceding set of options, one may choose to have no table between the parties (See Figure 4). This is a very open, informal setting, best used to maintain the close relationship between parties who have little need for writing, a maximum need to interact, and who both feel safe.

Figure 3

Figure 4

Someone may be tempted to mediate from behind a desk, with the parties on the other side, or with both parties on the same side of a table. Both situations present significant risks. Mediator mobility is minimized and the parties' access to each other is maximized. Behind a desk, the mediator may be perceived to be aloof. In Figure 5, the parties show signs of agitation, and the mediator has responded by standing up. By the time the mediator can get to the front of the desk (Figure 6), the parties have already moved. Settings like these should be avoided.

Figure 5

Figure 6

Figure 7

Sofas are another option for an informal setting. They seat the parties in the same position, facing the same direction. The parties are perhaps being subtly requested to look at things from the same point of view, but are discouraged from looking at one another, as to do this requires sitting in ways that the sofa does not encourage, i.e., with the knees drawn up, the torso twisted and resting in the corner of the sofa. Writing is not encouraged by the use of sofas. There are no barriers between the clients. Figure 7 shows a setting characterized by a couch.

Chairs can contribute to the ambiance of the situation. The atmosphere can be manipulated by increasing the firmness of the chairs to make the situation more formal or business-like, so that people must sit up and therefore be perhaps more alert. Making cushions softer encourages clients to relax and open. Facing the chairs toward each other encourages people to converse, while facing them towards a third person encourages conversation with that person and discourages other interchanges. Large chairs may give people a sense of authority, while small chairs make people feel more insecure.

The Room

Room size, the location of exits, color and decor are major considerations. Small rooms tend to make men more cantankerous and women more accommodating.[2] Small rooms tend to be stuffier and may seem to close in on the clients if they lack mirrors, contain too much furniture or are painted in dark colors. Ideally, two rooms should be available, one small and one larger. This allows the mediator to increase the pressure to settle by choosing the appropriate room size, and also provides a place for caucusing. Different colors can also be selected for use in different situations. A pleasantly decorated room, neat and clean, is likely to increase the clients' perceptions of mediation as a pleasant way to resolve problems.[3]

The location of exits is an important safety consideration (see "Safety and Weapons"). However, even where the threat of danger is small, clearly marked and readily accessible routes of escape relax people, even though this response may be an unconscious one. Ideally, each room should have two exits so that the parties may exit separately.

Decor of the mediation room can range from office-like to home-like. Office environments contain a table, conservative furniture, probably chairs rather than sofas, a desk-height bargaining table and the other accoutrements of business-like atmospheres conducive to bargaining. Home-like environments are more likely to contain a couch, a less-imposing table and perhaps more plants. Decor should be chosen based upon the anticipated clientele. Business-related conflicts probably call for a business-like setting, while family conflicts are sometimes more easily settled in an informal atmosphere.

Mediator Attire

Attire communicates nonverbally to clients. It can increase or decrease perceived credibility and authority. It can similarly contribute to or reduce perceived levels of empathy. These effects are widely reported (see "The Language of the Body"). Generally, the best advice is to dress to resemble the clients if the goal is to establish a peer relationship. Dress more formally and more expensively to increase the perceived level of authority, but only if the possibility of sacrificing rapport is worth the risk. Nothing substitutes for a well-presented introduction and a deep familiarity with the role and techniques of mediation, but subtle influences of attire should not be over-looked.

Appearance also is affected by hair length and style, the use of makeup, and the like. The key consideration is to know the desired effect. Credibility is enhanced by both peer relationships and superior appearance. Peer relationships, encouraged by similarities in general attire and appearance, do not augment the mediator's control of the situation, but do encourage trust. Superior attire and general appearance may breed respect or contempt, in one whose feelings of inferiority are aroused. Research has revealed the complexity of these effects. Avoid oversimplification by being aware that no single cause will yield a consistent result. Flexibility is needed. It is, however, easier to "dress down" a formal look than to "dress up" an informal one when one has come to a session not knowing which look will provide the best results.

Conclusion

Creating the setting is an important consideration that should not be left to chance. Planning for safety and for the anticipated clientele can positively influence the outcome of the mediation. Failure to plan ahead can cause injury, reduce rates of resolution, and result in an evaluation by the clients that mediation is ineffective.

Notes

1. Burgoon, Judee Kand Saine, Thomas: *The Unspoken Dialogue: An Introduction to Nonverbal Communication* (Houghton Mifflin Co., Dallas, TX 1978), p. 135.
2. Ibid.
3. Burgoon & Saine, op. cit., p. 106.

V. Verbal Processes in Mediation

Before the recent concentration on unconscious body language as an important dimension of communication, the focus of most analysis was upon speech as the means to understand and settle conflicts. That both are important is now clear. Methods of analyzing both forms of "language" will be offered in this and a subsequent chapter. Mediators will thereby obtain skills in communicating with clients on both conscious and unconscious, verbal and non-verbal levels, and in understanding their communications. This section is intended to provide methods of analyzing the content (semantics) as well as the structure (syntax) of what is being said. Attention will be devoted to three processes: generalization, deletion, and distortion.[1] These subjects are very complex, yet a basic understanding will pay many dividends in mediator effectiveness.

Generalization

Generalization is a term which describes a phenomenon common in all language. Generalization occurs when a single event or a series of events is presumed to be an endlessly recurring phenomenon, treating the single occurrence as if it were predictive of all future occurrences. Generalization is a form of thinking that takes one event or series of events and composes a description of experience based solely upon that event. For example, suppose two clients are talking. Here is an example.

Client one: "You didn't say that!"
Client two: "You never listen!"
Client one: "You are always saying that about me."
Client two: "I've never lied to anyone."

Temporal Generalization

Client two generalizes in line two. "Never", like "always", is a long time. In fact, Client one demonstrates that he listened, however inaccurately, simply by virtue of having responded in the context of the conversation, as demonstrated by the response of Client two. "Always" and "never" occur throughout the selected portion, and are good indicators of the occurrences of generalizations. Let us call this form of generalization a "temporal" generalization.

There are other, perhaps more subtle indicators of the use of generalization.

Client one: "Last week, you did not do the dishes like you said you would. Naturally, when you said yesterday that you would do the dishes tomorrow, I didn't believe you."
Client two: "When we got married, you said you'd never ask me to do the dishes. What else did you promise that you'll ignore?"

The generalization by Client one is a misuse of a form of inductive logic. Client one proceeds from the occurrence of an event to the belief that the event will continue to occur. Client two proceeds likewise, using a question to make a declarative statement. This form of generalization can be called an "inductive generalized fallacy."

Causal Generalization

Another form of generalization derives from the connection of unrelated events into a pattern. For example, someone is habitually late, always arriving fifteen to thirty minutes behind schedule. The reasons have been, "I forgot to shave" or, "I got a telephone call." Here is another conversation that a mediator hears:

Client one: "You're always late! Last night you got to the party when it was almost over. You're always taking two hours to shave or some such thing!"

Client two: "I was in an automobile accident three hours before the party began and I had to go to the hospital. Do you want proof? I can supply it."

In this instance, client one believed that another occurrence of tardiness had taken place. But the meaning of the event in question has a close connection with intent. Intent implies a willingness/unwillingness or an ability/inability. Client two may have a willingness to ignore time commitments and/or an inability to meet those commitments. But in the case of the automobile accident, the pattern probably does not apply. This form of fallacy can be termed "causally misconstrued" generalization.

Displacement Generalization

People often infer from their experience of causal events that responsibility falls upon the person who initiated the chain of events leading to the problem being discussed. This form of generalization can be called a "generalization of responsible displacement." For example:

Client one: "My car was parked in a fifteen-minute zone. I had plenty of time to finish my business with you but you screwed up the check. I got a ticket because of your screw-up. People who cause problems should pay for them!"

Client two: "Mistakes happen. You should have gone outside and put more money in the meter!"

The generalization is "people who cause problems." The misplacement is in the assignment of responsibility merely from participation in a causal chain. Causal chains are virtually endless. Thus the meaning of "cause" in this context needs to be specified. The generalization is expressed by the lack of specific reference.

Inspecific Generalization

Generalization also occurs in a broader variety of cases where there is a lack of specificity in the nouns or verb processes. Let us term these "generalizations of inspecificity." "Specificity" means that the sentence makes reference to a single identifiable entity or set of entities, or to a single process or set of processes among events. "Inspecificity" is a failure to specify. If someone says,

"He did it!," there are two unspecified nouns—"he" and "it," and an unspecified process from the verb "to do." Who is "he" and what was "done"? Listen to the following conversations and try to pick out generalizations. The mediator will point out some, but not all of them.

Client: "Sure, I'll tell you what happened. I went home that night and saw them on the couch. They was getting ready for something, I'll say."
Mediator: "Who was on the couch?"
Client: "The two of them were going at it."
Mediator: "Who, specifically?"
Client: "My girlfriend and Don."
Mediator: "Were they getting sexual with one another?"
Client: "Yeah, they always do. She never was interested in me."
Mediator: "When was this?"
Client: "The other day. I was O.K., until she started seeing him."

You should be able to notice words like "something," "they," "it," "always," "never," "O.K." and phrases like "the other day" and that night." These are nouns and phrases which lack clear references to experiences that the client has had. The client has used nouns in a general way when they were meant to refer to specific instances. Similarly, the client has used verbs and verb phrases in vague ways. For example, "doing it" may refer to sexual foreplay, sexual intercourse or even cooking dinner or playing croquet, although the slang expression often refers exclusively to sexual events. "Getting ready" is similarly vague. That phrase can refer to disrobing or petting.

Knowing the four categories of specific generalizations and the one general category gives you a structure by which to ask questions that challenge the client's generalized forms, as the last dialogue illustrated. Of course, there are often more questions that need to be asked than the client can handle all at once.

Deletion

In addition to generalizing, clients will delete important information. The information will be about who, what, when, where, why and how. These categories are often deleted from what clients will say about their experiences and observations. "Experience" constitutes the raw data from which a map of all aspects of the experience can be drawn. The language actually used is a map of the map, or a "meta-map," since what is uttered cannot duplicate in its entirety the experience itself nor the experience of the experience, the map. The map deletes many aspects of the experience. The map talks about feelings experienced, and may even evoke them, but the experience as such is already past and cannot be retrieved in its entirety. The meta-map makes further deletions, because memory is faulty, because the client lacks the skills by which to structure the experience for the map, or just to save time.

Memory can be stimulated by the appropriate questions from the mediator. The memory search can be guided by using the client's predominant sensory cues, as discussed in more detail below. For example, the mediator can ask the client to "look for" or "recall" the information. The mediator can, by having reconstructed the time sequences and by using "natural logic" (the commonly occurring forms of sorting information into temporal and causal sequences), help reconstruct what happened. For example, knowing that event "A" occurred at 9:00 A. M. and knowing that event "B" occurred after event "A," we know that event "B" occurred after 9:00 A. M. Unfortunately, natural logic may also lead us to believe that when a person trips over a roller skate and falls, that the roller skate caused the person to fall.

Natural logic cannot be explored in detail here, but let us explore by means of a dialogue and its natural logic and the concept of deletion.

1. Client: "I'm afraid." . . . (hesitates)
2. Mediator: "You're afraid of (what) (whom)?"
3. Client: "I'm afraid that they're going to leave the apartment."
4. Mediator: "What would happen if they did leave?"
5. Client: "Where would I get the money?"
6. Mediator: "The money for what?"
7. Client: "The mortgage. It's $800.00."

Notice that in the first sentence, the client deletes information about what he is afraid of, who is the source of the fear, and why that fear exists. The mediator decides to ask about "what" the client is afraid of in the hopes of getting the client to fill in the deleted material.

In the third line, the client beings to fill in portions of the map that were deleted from the meta-map. The mediator chooses to find out about the consequences that would follow. The mediator could also have asked about the rental unit and perhaps more about the nature of the relationship between the clients.

The client is experiencing stress, perhaps due to an inability to fully structure the experience of having a renter move out. The mediator can probably ignore the lack of structure suggested by the expression of fear. To explore that might probe far beyond the immediate issue. We must continue to explore the client's structure for producing alternatives, helping to establish their perception. Follow this conversation further:

1. Mediator: "When is the next mortgage payment due?"
2. Client: "On the 15th."
3. Mediator: "So you have 20 days."
4. Client: "Yes."
5. Mediator: "What can you do in the next 20 days?"
6. Client: "I could rent the apartment, of course. But they've left the place in a mess. They should have to pay for that."
7. Mediator: "How much damage has there been?"

In line one, the mediator asks for some information not supplied to that point (and thus deleted from the meta-map) by the client. Naturally, the client might have supplied that information in the next breath. From the client's response, the mediator draws a simple conclusion, to which the client assents. In line five, the mediator again seeks to fill in information not yet supplied, calling upon the client's logic. In line six, the client fills in the information, this time without prompting from the mediator, about the consequences flowing from the obvious rental option. The mediation then asks the client for an assessment of the damage.

1. Client: "The best estimate was for $600.00."
2. Mediator: "Best?"
3. Client: "The least expensive of the three."
4. Mediator: "Did all three estimators offer to make the same set of repairs?"
5. Client: "Ah, . . . yes, I think so." (Shrugs)

In line one, the client used a term of comparison (best) but deleted the point of reference. We know by reference to natural logic that best has to be best according to a basis of comparison. The mediator challenged the comparative term in line two, looking for the basis being used. Let us continue.

Mediator: "You're not sure?"
Client: "I have to assume so."
Mediator: "Do you have to check it out, or should you decide on how much money you want without knowing for sure?"
Client: "Well, I guess I'll settle for that much. If I get even half that, I'll consider myself lucky."

The challenge produced a statement revealing that the client felt forced to do something ("have to assume"). The mediator could have attempted to find out why the client was responding to the experience in that way; e.g., who or what is forcing you to assume precisely which assertion, and what would happen if the client did not make the assumption? Often a sentence will contain more than one item of deleted data, among which the mediator must choose. The basis for determining the line of questioning must derive from the mediator's sense of what is most appropriate for the progress of the mediation.

Unspecified forms of comparison; i.e., better, best, longer, taller, fatter, and so on, are unclear in two basic ways. First, what is often deleted is the person or thing which forms the object of comparison. The mediator can obtain a fuller understanding by getting the client to fill in what is deleted. Second, people not only will often delete the object of comparison, but the basis of comparison as well. To say simply that something or someone is better than "x" does not tell the listener *why*. The mediator can often discover important facts about the experience of the client by searching for the rationalizations employed by the client. A word of caution is necessary. People will often defend themselves from questioning when they are threatened into revealing information about which they are sensitive. When you notice a client becoming hostile towards you or reacting to questions in ways that reveal anxiety, proceed only with caution or pursue a different tact.

Distortion

Another problem people encounter in moving from experience to the meta-map can be termed distortion. Two forms of distortion, nominalization and presupposition, will be discussed. Nominalization is defined as making a reference to a process using a noun (usually a noun ending in -tion). For example, when we refer to mediation as such we are nominalizing. To refer to mediation in a way that takes into account its nature as a process, we should use the term "mediating," which we formulated by making the participle of the verb "to mediate." The participle is used gramatically to refer to on-going processes (he was mediating, he is mediating, he will be mediating, etc.) Nominalizing suggests the attempt to make something final when it is on-going. Let us continue with the dialogue:

Mediator: "So you would settle for $300.00?"
Client: "I think that negotiation is always like that."
Mediator: "Is it worth trying for $600.00?"
Client: "May as well. Nothing to lose if there is a resolution."
Mediator: "What if they don't go for that amount right away?"

The client nominalized "negotiation" in line two. Negotiation is clearly a process, but the client has a fixed idea of what it is like. We see once again the word "always," which emphasizes a static quality. The mediator responds by communicating a dynamic quality, thus encouraging the perception of the dynamic nature of the process. In line five the client nominalized "resolution." The mediator indicated the need to go through the process of resolving by asking the client a "what if" question, encouraging the client to think about the steps required to achieve the goal.

The mediator in both cases responded to the client's attempt to delete the experience of process from the map or meta-map. The client presumably has the experience of processing interpersonal disputes. Yet that experience did not make its way to the meta-map. Either of two reasons can explain the deletion. First, a distortion of experience can take place. During the experience, the reticular system (which is a brain function that filters information) may choose to filter out the experience of negotiation as a process. The filtration would prevent the information from being entered into the map. In this instance, the client's reticular system has allowed only limited and negative experiences of negotiation to enter. In instances of this sort, the mediator may not have the time nor the skills to fully remedy the problem, but he can nonetheless make an effort to provide examples of settlements where both parties win or other pleasant expressions of the process in which the client is engaged.

Nominalization can also take place as a result of a distortion of the map. In this instance, the client experienced the process nature of the experience and made a representation of that experience, but omitted that representation from the meta-map. The mediator's questions can help the client rediscover the representation, thereby helping to increase the options that are effectively available.

Presuppositions are also a form of distortion. Many things that we say presuppose something else which we fail to mention. For example, when we say, "This is a mess. Juan must have been here again," it must be true that Juan is messy. Similarly, "You know how tenants are, never on time with the rent," one presupposes that tenants indeed are never on time with the rent and that you know about this. For example, follow the continuation of the dialogue:

Client: "Well, you know how tenants are. They never accept the first offer. They can't pay anyway. I'd better start with $900.00."
Mediator: "Tell me how tenants are." (Alternately, and less likely to be viewed as hostile: "You've always have had bad experiences with tenants?")
Client: "Yeah, they're always trying to get more out of you than they deserve."
Mediator: "Always?"
Client: "Well, most of the time."

In Line one, the client presupposed that a characteristic of some tenants generalizes into a truth about all tenants. The mediator challenged this presupposition in Line two. The client continued the assertion in Line three. The mediator then repeated the challenge and succeeded in getting the client to recognize the distortion.

On the following pages is a dialogue, the client's portion is on the left, the mediator's is on the right. The mediator's response sometimes indicates the problem expressed by the client. In some statements, more than one problem has been referred to.

The purpose of the dialogue is to allow you to exercise your own choices regarding the client's statements by supplying possible mediator responses. After you have made your own response to the client's statement, look in the right hand column to find out what was actually chosen as the response. The point is not to argue that only one response is possible or best, but to encourage you to begin to exercise more choices in your responses. The mediator's statement or question presents only one possible response. After you have read the client's statement and made your own response(s), and have read the actual response, proceed to the next statement by the client and repeat the process.

C = Client

M = Mediator

C—I am glad you could find time to talk to me. I have some serious problems I want to talk about. . . . (hesitates)

M—Yes?

C—Well, she is always doing this to me!

M—(Always) Doing what?

C—Filing for divorce, and blaming me. (becomes teary)

M—(Blaming you for what?) When did she file?

C—Well, first about two years ago, and that's when I started seeing another woman.

M—Do you continue seeing the other woman? (Who is the woman?)

C—We got back together again so I stopped seeing her for a while.

M—How did you decide to get back together again? (How long did you continue without seeing the other woman?)

C—Well, we agreed that if I would stop seeing her, she would start being more affectionate. Hah! She never does that and wouldn't know how! She would make an ice cap seem warm! She forced me back to my girlfriend.

M—She *made* you go back to the girlfriend? (Causally misconstrued generalization)

C—Yes, so I started to see my old girl friend again.

M—How would you like your wife to be? (refer to "she never does that")

C—Well, I would like her to talk to me in a voice that does not sound like a lumberjack. She booms like a drill sargeant. She never touches me.

M—Would you like her to touch you more? (Checking the kinesthetic response.)

C—Yeah, I want her to touch me (winces).

M—But mostly you wanted her to talk differently?

45

C—Yeah, and if she would say something nice to my friends once in a while. Such a gruff tone.

M—What did she say to you this last time when she told you that she wanted a divorce.

C—She yelled, "I'm going to divorce you, you _____!" My divorce is going to be painful, I'll tell you.

M—Divorcing is always painful? (nominalization)

C—No, divorcing does not have to be painful.

M—Why did you say it was going to be painful?

C—I guess I just sort of assumed it would be. Everything else with that woman has been.

M—Everything? (generalization)

C—Well, no, when we were younger, we used to have lots of fun.

M—What have you done that you both enjoyed? (Lots?)

C—We went to a nice restaurant and had a glass or two of a nice wine. We both felt really good.

When? (Deletion)

C—This was just after we got back together after she filed the first time. What could be better?

M—I don't know. What do you think? (deletion)

C—Well, yeah, getting along better all the time would be better.

M—How would getting along be better? (comparative deleted)

C—Well, I wouldn't be having to pay an attorney.

M—How is that good? (deletion of how)

C—I want to save money. Not just on attorneys, but I've got property and she'll want it all. She didn't put together this fortune, I did! I'll support her well, very well, but not everything!

M—What is the composition of your fortune? (deletion—what; "all"—how do you know?; deletion—only you put together the fortune?)

C—There's about _____ pieces of property. They're all paid for.

C—I do not know how much they'd actually bring in this market.

M—What is the worth of the property, in your opinion?

C—I guess we could get a market analysis done by respectable folks.

M—How could you find out? (Deletion that was recognized—"I don't know.")

C—She didn't say she wanted it all. She just said she was going to get me. I know she wants it all!

M—What did she say she wanted from you? (deletion made earlier)

C—I don't remember what she looked like when she said that. But if it hadn't been for her, I'd be a happy man today.

M—What did she look like when she told you about her intent to divorce you this last time?

C—Of course I'd be happy. I married her and I was happy and now I'm not. You know how women are!

M—You'd be happy if you had never met her.

NLP: Modes of Thought[2]

Neuro-linguistic programming (NLP) offers several systematic approaches to the study of personal change. Among these are the study of pace, anchors (a la Pavlov), therapeutic metaphors and sensory modes. In this final section, we will discuss only this last category. Understanding Neuro-Linguistic Programming provides skills in persuasion necessary to a mediator.

Visual

Vision is a predominant sense. Most people experience their thoughts eidetically. They "picture" what is being said or done. Thus, they may translate auditory and kinesthetic data into imagery and then transfer that experience into words, actions, or more pictures.

Visual thinkers can be identified by eye movements or by audible cues. The eye movements for visual types are as follows: 1) looking up and to the right, signifying a memory search, or 2) up and to the left, signifying the creation of a new image. These directions are reversed for some people, but only a very small percentage of this behavior is random (remember, the eyes are truly the gateway to the brain). The meaning of the pattern can be established by skillful questioning. For example, if you ask a visually oriented person about a past event (i.e., an early childhood memory), and you notice that the eyes went up and to the right, and this pattern is repeated as a consequence of similar questions, a pattern has been established.

Visual thinkers can also be identified by the use of visual phraseology in their speech. They "look at" what you are saying, have a "clear image" of the situation. I met a musician the other night who came into the audience to "see" how the music sounded!

Auditory-digital

People who think mostly in words constitute the next most populous category, whose title signifies the powerful link between audition and logic. The auditory-digital thinker, too, can be identified by eye movements and auditory cues. Eye movements typically proceed from side to side. These are the "shifty-eyed fast talkers" you may have discovered in your reading who "wouldn't look you in the eye". Their speech is full of reference to sound, tones and the like. Do you *hear* what I am saying to you?

Kinesthetic

Have lots of feelings, "heavy" or otherwise? Tend to look *down* and away from people? Sensitive and easily hurt or excited? If this fits you, perhaps you are kinesthetically oriented. Notice children when they are reprimanded. Do they look down? Has anyone ever said to you in anger (kinesis), "Oh, come on!" Speech patterns and eye movements are powerful indicators of the thinking mode.

Everyone combines these modes into patterns. For example, someone may look up (visualizing) when you speak to him, then look down before talking to you. In that time, he has processed what you said in a visual-kinesthetic-auditory pattern. Discovering these patterns can assist you to understand the processes your client went through in coming to the conclusions about the experience under consideration. Utilizing this knowledge can help you to achieve better rapport and communication through mimicry. For example, if someone is visually oriented, you can use visual cues in your speech patterns. If the client says, "It looks to me like . . ." you can respond with, "What is the picture you are getting?" In this example, the predicates are congruous ("looks" and "are getting"). Similarly, if the client looks down (kinesthetic) and then says, "It looks to me like . . . ", you may respond by saying, "How do you feel about what you are seeing?" Mixing modes like this should be done carefully, however, as the individual is sometimes not conscious of his kinesthetic response. Making reference to feelings (or other unconscious modes of thought) sometimes confuses the client or otherwise hinders communication.

In this chapter, generalization, deletion, distortion and modes of thought have been examined. Careful study of this exposition, combined with intense practice in listening and questioning, creates powerful persuaders. Most of the material is intuitively obvious. However, careful attention to the statements of people you regularly meet should provide additional experience by which to augment awareness.

No communication method is fool-proof. Complications inevitably set in. What do you do with a person who mixes his modal strategies, for example, or with a person whose statements are very confused, or in situations in which the statements come so fast that the brain gets overloaded? Dealing with problems like these requires additional preparation, which may be obtained by reference to books on N.L.P. listed in the bibliography.

The Use of Questioning

In this chapter, we will discuss techniques of questioning. Here, instead of examining methods of asking questions to clarify what the speaker has said, we will discuss the use of questioning to help clients evaluate both outcomes and reasoning. The successful development of this skill can make the difference between a successful and unsuccessful mediator.

Purposes

There are several purposes for making use of questioning. First, questions help to reveal what the client knows about a situation, event or person. For example, asking the automobile repair shop owner about the cause of engine back-firing can reveal, to the mediator who understands automobiles, if the shop owner knows the correct answers. Similarly, if the client is a tenant seeking the return of a security deposit, does he know what the terms and conditions for the return are?

Secondly, the mediator can ask questions to determine the bases for the client's demands. Many people know what they want, but their reasoning does not always sustain the conclusion they have reached. One of the purposes of questioning is to determine how well-founded the client's position is.

Third, questions can establish the client's understanding of the opponent's positions. Normally, most people invest the majority of their resources coming to conclusions about their own needs and wants. Rigid ideas about fairness contribute to rigid stances that exclude the needs of others. Questioning can reveal to the client what he knows about the other side.

Fourth, questions can clarify that the client has heard and understood what has been said. The mediator can lead the client through the techniques of active listening. By asking the client to repeat what has been said, and by asking questions to reveal that understanding has taken place, the mediator can determine that the client is ready to move on in the conversation. For example, a client's wife has made an offer to give him $15,000 in cash, plus $500 per month for five months for his share in the equity in their house. The mediator asks "What was the offer she just made?" Jim responds, "Well, she offered me $15,000 in cash plus $500 a month for my share of the house. The mediator then asks, "$500 per month for how long?" If Jim says, "Oh, ah, 6 months, I believe," the mediator will ask Jane, "How many months did you say?" Jame will say "five months," and the mediator will say "So that's $2500." Jane will agree, and John will then know exactly what Jane has offered him.

Active listening not only helps clarify what has been said for everyone, but an active listener also develops a good rapport with his clients. Good active listeners convey the impression of caring for and understanding others.

A fifth purpose fulfilled by questioning is to gauge the strength of the parties' commitment to resolving the problem. Questions that go unanswered have either not been thought about or can not be answered by that client. Answers that miss the point or only partially answer the question may reveal a tendency to avoid the question. Indications of weakness in the argument can be discovered, as can a half-hearted intent to resolve the problem. A person who does not have an answer, or has only a partial one, and who is unwilling to work to find answers, may not be dedicated to resolving the conflict.

A sixth purpose is the discovery of consequences, the "what if" referred to elsewhere in this book. By asking questions, the mediator can help the client to discover the consequences and relative merits of various alternatives. How much will a lawyer cost? How much time will a court hearing take? How much risk do you face if you do not respond to your husband's demands? People in conflict often need assistance in thinking through their problems. We are each confined to the perspectives we define as possible. As one Buddhist saying puts it, "Being within the house, we see it not." Having someone from the outside help us think through the problems we face without judging or forcing us to defend positions that may or not be in our best interest, the nonjudgmental questioner helps keep people flexible by allowing them maneuvering room and easy, face-saving changes.

A seventh purpose emerges from the questioner's ability to keep the conversation moving. People who sit silently have the opportunity to shore up their own position. Having to answer questions helps prevent this, while at the same time furrowing the ground to make it fertile for new ideas.

From this emerges an eighth purpose. By maintaining the flow of questions, the mediator maximizes the ability to control the argument. "The one who controls the questions also controls the answers," says a common slogan. The control the mediator seeks is over the parties' tendency to avoid, confuse and deny the issues, and the proclivity to file suit over even very minor problems.

These eight major purposes of questioning can be accomplished by the techniques outlined in the chapter on "Verbal Processes in Mediation." In addition, however, we must add techniques to assure that a good rapport is assured by the questioning technique. Furthermore, we must develop methods whereby we can help people develop new ideas about problems that have probably worn them thin.

Active Listening

Active listening is comprised of questions and declarative statements. Good active listeners send "I" messages instead of "you" messages. A good active listener gives feedback to the speaker, either in declarative or interrogatory form.

"She never listens to me!" said the client. The mediator responded, "Are you saying that she is always ignoring you?" The active listener will combine questions and declarations, and will sometimes use the exact words the speaker just used.

A good listener will remember what has been said all along by developing a capable memory, a good understanding of what has been said, and a good note-taking system. One should be able to describe with accuracy the details of a problem or a solution. He must be well-organized enough to remember large volumes of information and distribute that information when it is needed. Subsequently, the active listener must also be a good questioner who can clarify statements of fact and argument with the correct probe.

Logic

Logic plays an important part in questioning. Logic leads us to the discovery of inconsistency, impossibilities and unanswered questions. We know that a person can not be in two places at once, pay more bills than he has money to pay with, both totally love and totally hate someone, be on time and late simultaneously, etc. Logic tells us that arguments *ad hominem,* appeal to authority and the other Aristotelean classes of invalid arguments, reveal beliefs that are not sustainable under questioning. Often, people do not trust possible solutions because their adversary has offered them. The questioner seeks to find out whether the solution will be acceptable regardless of whether the person who offered the solution is acceptable. To the person who asks, "Why should I trust him?," the questioner can respond, "What would be required to assure you that his promises will come about?"

Logic informs us of the basic relationship between time and the sequence of wants. In listening to clients speak, the questioner can begin to construct a map of what event happened at which time. The events should flow from each other. Events that cause others must precede them in time.

However, not all apparent causal events are really causal. Asking the speaker how he knows that an event caused another one should reveal the speaker's actual understanding of the relationship between the events.

Plato's dialogues exemplify some of the most skillful questioning ever recorded. Socrates seeks through his questions to lead the speaker through the argument independent from individuals. The good questioner does not seek any outcome except the one the logic of the situation demands. The questioner becomes separate from the question and the answers to which they lead, and avoids personalizing the task.

The Rational Agent

Many questioners assume that a person naturally seeks to operate in his best interest. In studying a person's actions, the mediator asks what would each party have to gain, and what would each have to lose, by pursuing a given course of action. Some people assume that, even though a given course of action is causing a person harm, the harmed person is gaining something. The questioner seeks to uncover the motive, be it revenge, victory at all costs or some other deeply hidden desire.

What If

This single phrase leads into a question that can open a person to possibilities previously unavailable. "What if" questions explore future possibilities. Since they are directed to the client, they involve the client in the evaluation of the consequences which derive from the various options being considered. So doing helps the client to "buy into" the outcome that is ultimately achieved, and in addition, stimulates each client to think of future remedies and not past transgressions.

Knowing what the future might bring, governs the choices we make in the present. Some outcomes are more predictable than others. Total certainty is probably not possible. Some people assert high degrees of certainty about various outcomes. "If I go to court, I will win." "How do you know?" is an appropriate first response. "If I give him the money I owe, he won't stop bothering me." "Will he stop bothering you if you don't give him the money?," is a possible response. Or, "What if you give him part of the money now and part in one month if his behavior is adequate at that time?"

Uncertainty about outcomes can be handled by asking questions which probe for perceptions, probability and motivation. In questioning the clients' evaluation of the likelihood that outcome "x" will be stable, the mediator can ask, "How likely is that solution to work?," which can be followed with "What if the solution doesn't work?" If the major consideration is the performance of the other side, the mediator can ask the client to discover motivations for his opponent's compliance. If a person can be motivated to perform because of some incentive, then the likelihood of compliance increases.

Few things in life are certain. The question, "How certain would you like to be?" can help reveal the truth of this observation. Similarly, one can ask, "How much certainty is needed?," and how is this certainty to be achieved before a deal can be made. Often, certainty has a cost associated with it. The questioner can determine this cost.

Maintaining Rapport

In addition to active listening, there are several things one can do and several which one must not do to maintain rapport during questioning. First, questions should be phrased so that the mediator appears to challenge but not oppose the speaker. This can be accomplished by forming questions using non-hostile phrases and non-verbal communiques such as timing and the miming of the clients' non-verbal behavior. Questions which ask "how" offer the client a chance to explain without feeling attacked by the questioner.

Second, the questioner should send "I" messages, rather than "you" messages. "You" messages tend to be accusatory in nature, though perhaps only partly intentionally or a matter of intent and vocalics. "I" messages communicate less hostility and do not suggest the transfer of responsibility. The cornered person is usually less changeable than the one who feels he has room to maneuver. Following are examples of "I" and "You" messages:

Mediator: "I hear you saying that you want the house." ("I" message)
Wife: "See, I think he should move out."
Mediator: "You mean you want him to just move out?" ("You" message, where an "I" response should have been given.) Better:
Mediator: "I understand that you want *him* to leave?"

The questioner must become aware of what he is communicating nonverbally. Avoid tensing muscles or face and other actions that suggest tension or hostility. Sufficient eye contact to assure the speaker that he is being heard and not avoided must be maintained. On the other hand, the questioner must avoid over-gazing, which makes people nervous. He must be sensitive to nonverbal cues. Questions should be adjusted to encourage the client to relax and feel comfortable and safe. Periods of intense questioning must be broken up by talking about topics that are easily resolved. The questioner should praise his clients for the progress that is being made.

Phrasing the question appropriately also requires attention. Saying, "I hear you saying something ridiculous" is not acceptable, although this is an "I" message. The question is offensive. Appropriate questions avoid offending the client. Saying, "Have you stopped beating your wife yet?" is offensive, while "I understand that you are saying that you have beaten your wife in the past" is not so much so. Proper questioning requires sensitivity to a person's sex, age, color, creed, relative economic and social status, attitudes, interests, beliefs and so on. Avoid questions that reveal your own opinions, such as, "Don't you think you should stop beating her?," but find phraseology such as, "What if you continued beating your wife?," or "How will you avoid her retaliating if she chooses to do so?"

The questioner should also be aware of the likely answer. If for example, you are speaking with a wealthy person, asking about the costs of collection of a $300 claim, you may get an answer that you do not want. "Yes, it may cost more than he owes me, but I don't care because I can afford to get this no good. . . ." Find out what is important to the client first, and then ask the question. For instance, suppose the client says that he is very busy closing business deals. You may then want to ask, "How much of your time ought you to spend to collect this debt?" By discovering what the client's wants, needs, intent and other values are, you can ask questions that expose the relative merits of the various options in terms that are *meaningful to the client,* though they might not be meaningful to you personally.

Conclusion

Appropriate use of questioning has eight major purposes. To achieve the goals which extend from these purposes is to achieve a settlement rather than an unsolved case. The careful questioner maintains rapport by asking questions which reveal the nature of the problem and of the parties to it. Questioning is a diplomatic task that requires care and effort to communicate respect and understanding. Avoiding the pitfalls of judgmental methods, the questioner helps the client to his evaluation of the problem and the alternatives available.

Notes

1. Bandler, Richard and John Grinder. *The Structure of Magic: A Book about Language and Therapy* (Vol. 1) Scribner, 1985.
2. Grinder, John. "Frogs Into Princes; Neuro-Linguistic Programming" *Real People,* 1979.

VI. Non-Verbal Processes in Mediation:

The Language of the Body

Nothing is more astounding than to realize that the body has a language of its own. The expression, "the language of the body," brings this realization to the fore, and is as shocking as if we were to say, "The body has a mind of its own." Body language (which is used here as the equivalent to the more generic term, "non-verbal communication") is as complex as its verbal counterpart. A good mediator watches people in an attempt to discover meaning in their gestures, postures, positions, how close and in what positions they interrelate, who gestures to whom, when and where. Much of the literature on body language attempts to translate from gesture, posture and position to language. To some extent, this is undesirable. As much is lost in the translation as is lost in describing a great painting. Nothing can replace seeing it. Nonetheless, good analysis can help a person become aware of the special characteristics of great paintings. We can and must obtain a full awareness of the language of the body.

What is the task when we study the language of the body? Burgoon and Saine[1] have gathered some statistics that reveal the scope of the problem, and help to point out the difficulty of interpreting body language:

1. Pei estimates that man is capable of 700,000 different physical signs.
2. Birdwhitstell estimates that the face alone is capable of producing 250,000 expressions.
3. Physiologists estimate that the musculature of the face permits over 20,000 different muscular configurations.
4. In a study of classroom behavior, Krout identified 5000 different gestures.
5. In therapeutic situations, Krout identified 5,000 distinct hand gestures alone that he believed to have verbal equivalents.

This chapter will outline some major features of bodily expression as associated with verbalized thoughts. First, some basic postures will be described, with as little reference to their interpretation as possible. The description of these postures will be followed by a brief definition of special studies of how people physically interact. A description of a strategy to allow the interpretation of what is being communicated follows this. Because the interpretation of body language is so complex, oversimplification is almost unavoidable in such perfunctory analysis. These examples are only starting points for such interpretation. (Note: In the photographs that follow, the models were instructed to portray the emotions suggested by the text.)

Some Major Features

The Face

The face commands the most significant portion of our attention when we are with others. Even the poker face communicates; i.e., the attempt to be inscrutable. We smile when we are happy (see figure 8), when we laugh, when we are being sarcastic (see figure 9), sometimes when we are angry, sometimes when we are about to execute an act of revenge. Our lips are tight (tense) when we smile, or are spread wide as we roar at the antics of Inspector Clousseau (See Figure 10.).

Clowns caricature the frowns that sometimes occur when we are amusing others, yet other times we frown in worry (see figure 11) or as we concentrate on a difficult problem (see figure 12). Others come to ask, "Why are you worried?", and we respond in surprise, "Do you think I'm worried?" Some people frown as they relax with a question (See Figure 13.).

Figure 8

Figure 9

Figure 10

Figure 11

Figure 12

Figure 13

Figure 14

A grimace is an expression of pain (See Figure 14.). The grimace involves more facial muscles than does the frown or the smile. Muscles around the lips, cheeks and jowls, and around the eyes and forehead are used. The pain can be emotional or physical, and its origin cannot be distinguished by observation alone. Sometimes the grimace is an expression of pleasure, such as in response to a bad pun.

Shoulders

Shoulders are usually in the field of vision when one looks at the face, and are less expressive than the face. The shoulders become square during excitement, alertness or other "up" moods. (See Figure 15.) Excitement can also occur during a hostile mood. Shoulders become relaxed and rounded during periods of comfort, depression and other "down" or calm moods (See Figure 16), and also as a result of poor health or body posture. These cannot always be readily distinguished

57

Figure 15

Figure 16

Figure 17

from one another. Shoulders are sometimes used to express assertiveness, when they are used to gesture towards another person (See Figure 17).

Torso

The torso carries most of the body's weight and thus conveys much of the overall body posture. A slumped torso expresses relaxation, depression and other "down" moods, as do the shoulders. Figure 18 illustrates a relaxed person, while Figure 19 depicts a depressed person. Can they be

Figure 18

Figure 19

Figure 20

Figure 21

visually distinguished? An erect torso indicates alertness, excitement and the like. Figure 20 illustrates a rigid, militaristic and argumentive person who is alert or excited. Can this person be distinguished from the one in Figure 21, who has just received some good news, on the basis of the position of the torso?

The torso sometimes carries a disproportionate amount of body weight. "Reading" the posture becomes even more difficult, as the tension in the muscles is more difficult to notice. The torso can also be used in aggressive or sexual postures. (See Figure 22.) The upper torso or abdomen is pushed out to be made more noticeable.

| Figure 22 | Figure 23 |

Hips

Hips are also accentuated in aggression either by placing the hands on them or jutting them forward by rotating the hip and putting a leg forward (See Figure 23). Placing the hands on the hips is a common indication of impatience, but it is also a way of relaxing the shoulders.

Hips also communicate in movement. The sexual sway is often noticeable as a way of communicating "availability," but one commonly errs in the superficial interpretation of that motion. Frequently, the hips sway minimally from side to side, but because the walker has increased the gait towards a run, the hips act more specifically as a pivot for the legs.

Legs

The legs communicate mostly by means of their relationship to one another; i.e., whether they are crossed or spread. Legs can be crossed at the knee or ankle. American women and European men often cross their legs so that they drape roughly perpendicular to the floor (See Figure 24). Women adopt this position sometimes out of modesty. American men place one ankle above the other knee, so that the crossed leg is parallel to the floor. American men may have adopted this position to heighten the distinction between the sexes. Interpreting these postures requires an investigation of culture that cannot be done here.

Seated people sometimes sway or jiggle their legs. The rate of movement seems directly proportional to the intensity of the experience that is occurring. Yet not all persons who sway their legs gently or who sit without moving any part of their body are necessarily relaxed. Obviously, people often sit rigidly when tense.

Figure 24

Hands

Next to the face, the hands are the most expressive portion of the body. Their prehensile character, multi-boned flexibility and strength combine to allow the hands to assume many shapes and positions. Their location at the end of the arm gives them range, which can be added to by the flexibility and strength of the shoulders, back and chest. Our chief concern is in their function as gesticulators. This function may be associated with words or may be independent (as in the gestures of a policeman directing traffic).

Like other non-verbal communication, gestures are subject to a wide range of interpretation, some of which are contradictory. Following are some commonly observed hand positions. Interpreting these positions is left for you to do by applying the strategy to be outlined. The terms ascribed to the positions are intended to be descriptive of the position without reference to the meaning. However, some positons could not be labelled without reference to meaning.

1. The steeple: the hands bridge and form a roof-like peak (Fig. 25).
2. The prayer: the hands are held together, thumbs crossed (Fig. 26).
3. Intertwined: fingers interlaced, palms touching or close (Fig. 27).
4. Stretched: fingers interlaced, palms away from body, fingers bent away from body (Fig. 28).
5. Cross: palm on palm, fingers of each hand perpendicular (Fig. 29).
6. Fist: (Fig. 30).
7. Hitchhiker/umpire: fist with thumb extended (Fig. 31).
8. Halt! flat palm extended away from body (Fig. 32).
9. Why?/Pleading: hand(s) flat, palms up (Fig. 33).
10. Denial: hands crossing one another with palms down (Fig. 34).
11. Welcome: hands pointing to entry, seat, etc. (Fig. 35).
12. Pointer: (Fig. 36).

Figure 25

Figure 26

Figure 27

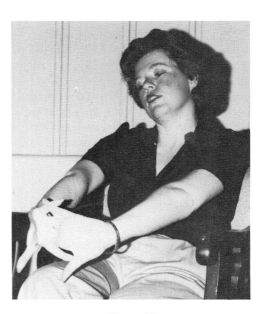

Figure 28

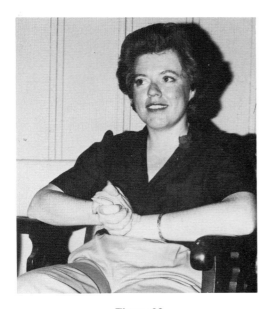

Figure 29

Figure 30

Figure 31

Figure 32

Figure 33

Figure 34

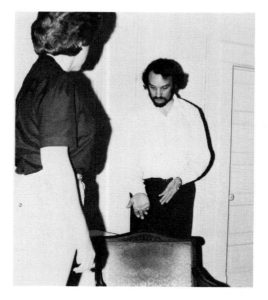

Figure 35

Figure 36

Many other gestures can be made with the hands, but no attempt to exhaust the topic will be made here. Many of these gestures, such as the welcome, denial and halt are readily interpreted. But others, like the hitchhiker/umpire, the steeple, and the prayer, are more difficult.

Body Postures

Gestures often occur together. The shoulders may be squared off, for example, while the hands seem to ask "Why?" (Fig. 37). The face may show a relaxed smile while the legs bounce nervously (Fig. 38). Or, a hand may be clenched while a torso slumps. The body speaks to us not only as individual parts but as a whole. The body moves or remains motionless. It leans back and forward, to the right and to the left. It is tense or relaxed. Its movements may be fluid or erratic. Some of its communiques are clearly sexual, some relay ambiguous sexual feelings, and some may seem to relay sexual messages but are actually indicating anger or frustration. All these meanings can be communicated by similar postures. What is the person saying in Figure 39?

Bodies communicate by their relative heights, shapes and weights. What do the figures in Figure 40 communicate to you? What do they communicate to some of your friends? Comparing the interpretations should be useful in producing a first-hand experience of the complexity of interpretations.

Figure 37

Figure 38

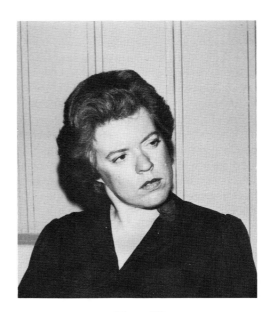

Figure 39

Figure 40

Figure 41

Figure 42

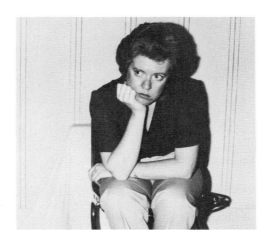

Figure 43

Figure 41 shows a person leaning forward with his eyes down. Is this a gesture of humility, is his back in pain or is he scratching his back? Figure 42 pictures a person leaning with his chin on his fist and his elbow on his knee. Figure 43 shows roughly the same posture. How would you compare the two figures? Why do they represent different things?

Haptics

The study of touching is called "haptics." Some people stand further from others and seldom touch. Other people will touch certain people but not others, or touch people in some situations, but not in other situations. Touching can be accidental, casual, initial, friendly, aggressive or intimate. Compare the handshake in Figure 44 with the one in Figure 45. Notice how much nearer

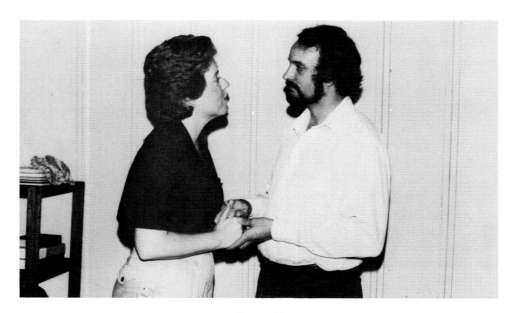

Figure 44

Figure 45

the couple is to each other in the former illustration. What other things do you notice? Can you conclude that the couple in Figure 44 has a closer relationship than the couple in Figure 45? Could it be that the people in Figure 40 are more intimate with one another?

In some instances, touching another person causes him to back up, leave, or get angry. At other times, touching brings about an opposite reaction. Variables such as cultural heritage, which cannot be observed in a single interaction, have been found to be very important in determining a person's response to touching.

Proximity

Proximity can be studied in combination with gesture and posture. We can stand close in gesture "x" and in posture "y," or more distant in gesture "a" and posture "b." For instance, two people can be close together with clenched fists and tense arms and legs, or more distant with no variation, or again close together with rounded smiles, closed eyes and gently curving outstretched arms. The formal study of proximity, called "proxemics," is an intricate discipline where studies are made of the relationship between how close people get to one another and the kind of personal relationship they have or do not have, their relative economic and social status, their dress, hair style, scent, their use of facial hair, hair style and length, the kinds of verbal messages being sent, expectations generated by previous contact. The list is a long one.

Where haptics is a study of touching, proxemics studies the distances people maintain between each other, and where gesturing and postures are studied to determine their function in non-verbal communication, the broad study of the situation in which these other concerns take place can give us many clues about the context in which non-verbal communication takes place. In order to interpret the language of the body, we have to study body language in its context. Thus we can not interpret the gestures of hands and legs without knowing more about the situation than what we merely see. For example, in figures 8, 9 and 10 we see people engaged in facial signals. In figure 8, the model was instructed to smile in happiness, in figure 9 in sarcasm and in figure 10 as if Inspector Clousseau had just stepped on his nemesis's finger as it poked through the floor. Either smile could be readily mistaken for the other. This often happens, as when the sensitive child or adult sees others smiling at him in mockery yet, when asked, maintain that they were laughing about the ignorant would-be football fan who went to the stadium expecting to get a quarter back in the form of a refund! Only the context of the situation can provide the correct answer. What were the people really smiling at? This is the type of question the people-watcher must ask.

A similar difficulty winds its way through all of the examples. Here is a list of questions you can use to help determine the context of the body language you are trying to interpret. Some of these questions have already been posed, but are placed here to make the list more complete and useful. Following each question is an additional assignment(s) for you to undertake to improve your understanding. Refer to the bibliography for sources of information.

1. What sex are the parties?
   Find out what relative inter-personal distances, room sizes, and the like that men and women prefer in given situations. Men, for instance, have been reported to be more cantankerous and women less so in restricted spaces (See Seine and Burgoon). We can more readily "invade" a person's "body space," a person's superior, or his subordinate?

2. What age are the parties?

   Do older people gesture more, less or differently than do younger ones? What effects do hierarchical considerations deriving from age have on determining proximity, touching or gesturing? Do children engage in as much gesticulation as do adults? In what ways do the gesticulations communicate different meanings, and how do these differences contribute to conflicts between adults and children?

3. What are the people doing in the situation?

   Are they at a party, a funeral, a shopping mall, in their car on a busy street, eating at a plain or fancy restaurant? What can you find out about their intentions; i.e., are they eating with an old friend or lover, or meeting someone they do not know well? What effects may these variables have upon their posture, gestures and so on?

4. What tone of voice or other vocal variations do you notice?

   Vocalics is the study of nonverbal components of utterances, such as harsh tones, squeaky voice, and stutter. What effects do you observe from various intonations and other variables? You may notice that a person who speaks in hushed tones causes people to lean forward to pay attention.

5. What are the speakers doing with their faces?

   This would include mouth, nose and eye shape, makeup, the manner in which their hair is arranged and whether they have facial hair. What effects do facial shapes have on people?

6. What shape do the shoulders have? The torso, legs, feet, hands, and general body posture? What seems to be the relationship between what is said and the body? Do you notice incongruities, perhaps someone saying "I like my job," while his hands are tense and his face in a grimace? Do you notice that one hand is tense and the other gliding gently back and forth? Find out about the sources of incongruities and what their occurrence might indicate about internal tension.

7. What seems to be the relationship between what is being said and the proximity and touching that is occurring?

   Do people seem to move apart or closer together as an indicator of levels of hostility? What are the vocal variations that go along with this movement?

Answers to questions like these are often required to interpret the language of the body. The most desirable strategy involves discovering the relevant facts about the situation (by asking the right questions) as they relate to the postures being studied. Only then can the posture, gesture or position be assigned meaning in the specific case. Then, observing these same postures may serve as a clue to the meaning of the situation when verbal cues are missing or in short supply. Knowing that an individual conveyed a particular meaning when performing a certain action in the past allows you to assume with some certainty that the meaning is the same in a subsequent occurrence.

Some universal body symbols do exist, and although most have more than one meaning per culture, their appearance can raise questions about the nature of the situation being observed. If you are speaking with two Arabs who are standing near each other, you should ask yourself why. If your American boss is doing the same thing, you should also ask why. The Arabs are probably friends, but the American may be exerting pressure of some kind.

The study of body language is complex. One is easily misled into misinterpretations by one's own errors as well as by the over-simplified popular literature on this subject. The generation of conflict through misinterpretations, as well as the correct interpretations of non-verbal communiques is well known. This chapter should put you on the road of increased sensitivity to what people are saying without their saying anything.

Caucusing Strategies

A caucus is simply a private discussion between the mediator and one of the parties to the dispute. Caucusing may occur during "across the table" mediations, or even when the parties do not sit down "face to face," as in conciliation. Caucusing can be used to gain information, increase or decrease tensions, or change tactics. These uses can be considered goals of caucusing, while the primary purpose of a caucus is to break deadlocks. A successful caucus must be introduced, the parties carefully prepared, and issues of timing addressed.

Definitional Nuances

As a private meeting between the mediator(s) and one side, a caucus constitutes a significant interruption or "change of pace" in a mediation session. It defines the "pace" of conciliation involving telephone or written contracts. Let us term the former sort of caucus a mediation caucus and the latter a conciliation caucus. In mediation, the caucus is clearly the intentional exclusion of one of the parties, and is not an accidental isolation of them. In the context of an accommodative process, this may seem ironic, since a coming together of the parties is a focal point of mediation.

Yet, a caucus can serve the achievement of consensus. It is a form of fractionating the conflict as it distinguishes issues.[1] Distinguishing issues (fractionating) helps divide a complex problem into more manageable portions. Separating the parties helps divide the affective and substantive contentions.

Ego needs and self esteem are often the issues of primary concern. These factors are present in conflicts involving neighbors, spouses, co-workers and contract disputes. Substantive issues are sometimes predominant in conflicts between businesses. But affective and substantive issues are always intertwined, even if the conflict does not begin with the personal focus. This stubborn fact reinforces the need for fractionating through caucus.

Affective themes are always difficult to manage, especially when they are a focal point of concern. The interactions that initiated the conflict are reproduced as the parties face one another in the mediator's presence. Separating the parties does not, in and of itself, resolve the problems in the transaction, but allows the mediator to reduce the number and intensity of transactions with the expectation of narrowing and identifying issues and possible solutions.

Substantive issues, such as how much, where, when and how can also be addressed in caucus. Often disputants can speak more honestly with no one present except the mediator. The caucus provides this opportunity. Sometimes an individual or group is not certain of the negotiating stance to adopt. The parties can "try out" different stances with the mediator. Internal uncertainty divides one side of a conflict within itself. This division can lead to greater complexities. The caucus is a means of obtaining internal consensus with each side separately.

Because substantive and affective issues are always intertwined, there is often more than one reason to caucus. If, for instance, a divorcing couple is having trouble dividing property, the problem may be due to the complexities of ownership and feelings arising from the sense of loss. Either of these issues may have called for a caucus, but combined, the issues necessitate a mechanism for reducing tension. The caucus is a way of untangling issues of how, and how much, from those of love or friendship.

In conciliation, the process of conflict resolution does not necessarily involve a meeting between the parties. Where no meeting is involved, the mediator is engaged in a caucus, whether by telephone, in person with one side, or by the mails. Thus, the main definitional difference between a mediation and a conciliation caucus results from the physical absence of at least one side, and either the physical presence of the other, or other form of direct contact with the mediator. Caucusing does not function as a mechanism for changing pace in the conciliation process since the conciliation process is a continuous caucus. There is no other major definitional difference between a mediation and a conciliation caucus, although there are implications for communication that arise from telephone and written contacts as distinguished from face-to-face meetings.

Tactical Concerns in the Mediation Caucus

Introducing the Caucus

The caucus must be discussed during the introduction to the mediation. By discussing the use of the caucus in the opening statement, the mediator avoids surprising or alarming the clients. The expectation that a private meeting may occur makes the caucus more palatable when it does happen, since the maneuver seems less like an unusual occurrence.

The clients must be assured that all parties will have an opportunity to meet with the mediator in caucus. This assurance helps maintain the impression of neutrality and fairness. One must be sure to meet with each side an equal amount of time, although saying this in the introduction is not necessary. "Equal time" enhances the credibility of the mediator as a neutral, since each side is being treated "the same."

Some mediators like to give reasons for the caucus and do so during the introduction. These reasons must be carefully constructed to avoid raising suspicions. Saying, "I will call a caucus so that people will be honest" may make people think that when the mediator does call the caucus, he is doing so because he is of the opinion that someone has not been honest. But there are many ways of stating the reasons for caucusing that avoid problems. For example, in discussing honesty, one might say, "Caucuses are useful in assuring frank exchanges." Similarly, speaking of tension reduction, one might say, ". . . if things are getting out of hand" or ". . . to help keep this easier for you." The mediator can frequently plead for such a meeting "to help me clarify my understanding."

Honesty and tension reduction are the only reasons that ordinarily should be discussed with clients. Tactical maneuvers probably need not be discussed if the maneuvers are to be effective.

Timing: Choosing When and Why

Knowing when to initiate a caucus is critical to its success. There are three major concerns, which if triggered individually or in combination, indicate the need for a caucus. These concerns are: 1) the need for information, 2) the need to affect tension levels and 3) the need to change approach with either or both sides.

The need for information manifests itself either in the demonstration of dishonesty or withholding. Dishonesty can be detected by logical examination or the client's construction of facts and circumstances, or by examination of the sentence structure to discover deletions, generalities and distortions. The same basic tactics apply to the discovery of withheld information. Many mediators have strong intuitions about honesty, intuitions that may arise from a peripheral grasp of the basic negotiating tactics being employed by the parties.

Once the mediator discovers that information is being withheld or distorted, and that questioning which avoids offending or embarrassing the clients is not going to yield the necessary information, a caucus is desirable to gather information. The relative importance of information must be determined by the "location" of the sought data in the sequence of transactions. For example, let us imagine that an automobile repairman is accused of having allowed one of his employees to use the other client's automobile for private purposes. The mediator discovered that the incident "may" have occurred. Then the mediator asks, "When did this occur?" The client might respond, saying "I do not know," or "Sometime last year." The client is responding vaguely (generalizing), and may be deleting or distorting information. This is a clue to the mediator that the client may need a private setting to discuss this matter. Because the issue is important in the sequence of transactions (i.e., the specificity is important to establishing the repairman's willingness to settle the issue), a caucus is justified.

Even in the absence of specific clues indicating withholding, deleting or distorting, the mediator may wish to caucus just to give the parties an opportunity to speak more honestly with the mediator. This opportunity should be taken if the mediator is not making progress toward resolution since not all suppressed information is manifested in behavior the mediator can interpret.

Tension levels can be increased or decreased with the caucus. Tension levels decrease when the parties' interactions are causing anxiety and hostility. Separating the parties reduces the rate at which they interact since the parties are not able to exchange audible communiques. But caucusing does not eliminate the interactions (playback or projection into the future) that continue to occur within each party.

Tension levels may increase as a result of psychological and physiological factors. Psychologically, the waiting party may begin to wonder what is happening. How long is the process going to take? What is the most likely final outcome? Thus, increased tensions result from the enhanced perception of uncertainty. Enhanced ambiguity can result from the questions of the mediator and generate subtle pressures for position examination. For example, the mediator questioning the repairman about the location of employees or their supervision could increase the client's level of tension.

This factor is amplified by a growing fatigue. The client's fears lengthen the perceived time elapsed for the waiting party. The body is increasingly drenched with the chemicals of stress. To varying degrees (which can be established through the interpretation of body language) rising levels of stress decrease the client's ability to resist change. The mediator must monitor the stress, since the stress must be discharged. How it is discharged is of critical importance. The difficulty that the mediator faces in monitoring the stress felt by the waiting client results from the bodily separation between the mediator and the waiting client. Monitoring must come from others assisting the mediator, an evaluation prior to the caucus (resulting in an estimate based upon the mediator's belief about the condition of the client and the effect of the passage of time on that condition), or a visit to the client. Visits or other "on site" checking should occur at a maximum of twenty minute intervals. Twenty minutes is also a desirable length for a mediation caucus.

The mediator seeks the discharge of stress which enhances the willingness to settle. A quick settlement at any cost is not the purpose of client stress management. Stress introduced by the mediator or by either of the parties is a part of the natural field of events in which mediation is encased. Yet the subsequent effects of stress upon the parties are a matter of the mediator's urgent concern. Rising tensions can create greater willingness to settle, provided the client does not get up and leave, become increasingly hostile to mediation or the mediator, or become too angry to be rational.

In short, stress must be managed so that it provides an animus to reexamination and settlement without causing damage. There are varying levels of threshold. Ideally, the mediator approaches the threshold without crossing the critical point of tolerance which would terminate the mediation. The mediator can continue to meet with the other client or stop to meet with the waiting client. The mediator can also provide refreshments to the waiting clients to temporarily reduce the tension. To continue to meet with the other may increase tensions, while the latter move should decrease tensions. During the caucus, the mediator should seek to uncover all sources of tension and decide whether to deal with them.

The level of tension can also be taken into consideration in choosing if or when to call a caucus. Reducing the tensions in the mediation room can be accomplished by calling for a break, calling for a caucus or continuing to work on the issues that are the source of tension. The reactions and intentions of clients are the critical factors. A party anxious to proceed may feel increased anxiety because a break was taken, while one who has become tired welcomes a break. Reactions to the calling of a caucus or the continuation of the mediation similarly vary. The mediator should assure that the rapport that has been built is enhanced by whichever option is chosen. If increasing the tension level produces higher motivation to construct an acceptable settlement, the mediator should make choices to achieve this result. If rising tension decreases this likelihood, the mediator may choose other options.

All interchanges demonstrate a relationship between tension, fatigue and the willingness to settle. But other factors also intrude into the decision-making matrix. One such factor derives from the changes in perception associated with caucusing and provides another rationale for calling a caucus. We know already that the caucus allows for frank exchanges and for increasing or decreasing levels of tensions. In addition, the caucus allows the mediator to treat each party individually and thus provides an opportunity to use tactics that more effectively communicate to a particular individual.

This communication change can take several forms. They are divisible into functional and neurological sorts. We each adopt various functional roles. For instance, we may be parental, childlike, a friendly guide, and/or an investigator. The mediator may choose these roles singly, in combination or in sequence. The personalities and interrelationships between the parties have powerful effects upon the choice of role. The caucus brings about a dramatic change since one party is no longer present. This condition permits the mediator to change roles. The mediator must make conscious, goal-oriented choices of roles. The major factors to consider are: the desired outcome of the caucus, the immediate state of mind of the participants, the levels of tension desired and achieved and the ability of the mediator to function in certain roles.

The desired outcome may be the establishment of greater rapport. If the mediator has been directive, then to acquire more trust and perhaps the establishment of peer pressure, the mediator can shift to the role of friendly assistant. This increased rapport can result in less damage, since the possible competitor is not present and the aura of neutrality can be retained despite excursions into what may seem to be overidentification with one side.

The client may be feeling very high levels of anxiety and isolation. Establishing a supportive relationship may not be possible in the presence of the other parties. Therefore, the mediator can call a caucus to create a non-directive parental character to give the client non-advocative guidance, perhaps through the analysis of costs and benefits. Such a change in mediator role usually produces a change in role selection by the client.

In instances where the client may be proceeding smugly without apparent tension, so confident of the outcome that little evidence of willingness to compromise or consider alternative solutions is seen, the mediator may wish to shift from a less assertive to a more interrogatory role. Using the caucus to make this transition has two advantages. First, the transition in role can be isolated in the caucus. Second, the new role may not be appropriate for both parties. The private meeting, in effect, allows the mediator to adopt two very different roles with the parties separated, and at least one additional role during the general session. Further flexibility is afforded when more than one caucus is called. Each transition may allow for tactical changes of the sort under discussion. The mediator must be cautioned to assure that the various roles are perceived as essentially cohesive, since a mediator who creates too diverse a set of roles may confuse his clients.

Exchanging the Parties

Where significant tensions exist, the mediator may be concerned about hostile exchanges. Care must be taken in instances of this sort to assure that the mediator retains control of the situation. There are two significant factors: the positioning of the mediator's body and the environment (chairs, tables, doors). Other factors come into play in crisis management.

The mediator must assure that in instances where one party will leave the caucus to be replaced by the other, the mediator must always be in control of the exchange. This can be accomplished if the mediator accompanies the party with whom he is finished to the waiting area, and then escorts the other party into the caucus room. Care must be taken upon leaving the room to exchange the parties, since if the waiting client is standing near the door, the client must either be moved away or the mediator must exit from the door first.

If a high likelihood of violence exists, placing the waiting party in a separate room could prevent difficulties in exiting from the mediation room. In addition, this arrangement would make exchanges easier to control, as the door would be replacing the mediator's body as the intended shield, leaving the mediator free to concentrate on things being said and done.

Having a room available in which waiting clients can sit in relative isolation also creates two other possibilities. First, it would allow for the use of two mediators, each caucusing with a client. There is no need for a client to be left alone at any time. Having continuous contact with a client is important when the client needs supervision. In addition, having two caucuses occurring simultaneously may save time. However, the mediators then have the task of communicating to one another about their respective meetings. Such communication is often exceptionally complex.

Shuttling

Throughout the whole process of settling the dispute, the mediator can exercise the option to remain in caucus for extended periods of time. Extended caucuses are more readily conducted when each client has a permanent room between which the mediator can shuttle back and forth without having to exchange the parties. The use of two rooms allows the parties to suffer fewer major moves, keep their paperwork in order, avoid one another, and reduces the mediator's anxiety concerning hostile exchanges.

Shuttling between the parties in this fashion is useful when the parties do not want to meet or when the mediator wants to keep them separate. "Hot" conflicts lend themselves to this technique, as do very complex cases involving powerful substantive and/or affective issues when the mediator perceives a need for frequent caucuses.

Shuttling can be combined with face-to-face mediation and conciliation to produce written or oral agreements. Except in the context of a face-to-face mediation (defined as a situation where the parties are in the same office or other similarly confined locality), shuttling is a form of conciliation. The nuances of the conciliation process, which is a perpetual caucus, will be discussed later.

Shuttling on the interpersonal or business level can also be conducted over long distances, and need not be confined to an office space. For example, a mediator may have one client in the office and another in a different city. While the client who is in the office waits, the mediator can discuss proposals with the other party by phone. Similarly, neither party need be in the same city as the mediator, who may handle the situation using the mails, telephone or, occasionally, other local mediators.

Handling problems through the mails poses some special problems, however, as written documents are involved. These documents can be collected and recorded as tangible evidence that can be judicially reviewed. If the mediator is using the mails, then great care must be taken to assure that information exchanged is either already documented by the parties (in which case the mediator is adding nothing tangible to the collection of evidence) or the mediator should transmit only arguments devoid of references to new data. In any case, substantive references must be avoided. Because of the risks to mediators and to the parties, written exchanges are a last resort tactic subject to the ethical review of the mediator. The mediator may decide that only the mails will make a resolution possible (say that one person is deaf and cannot engage in telephone conversations or is hospitalized in a distant city). In an instance of this sort, the mediator may have a moral obligation to take certain risks of involvement with the legal system. The existence of this moral obligation would depend on part on a distinction between positive and natural laws, since if there were no such distinction, the mediator might be more inclined to want to exercise only *legal* obligations.

Conciliation Caucuses

Where shuttling is involved in the course of a mediation, it is legitimately a "mediation" caucus. When the persons are not in the same building or are located at a distance such that the mediator cannot meet physically with both parties several times easily in the course of a day, the shuttling takes place in the context of a conciliation caucus. In fact, the terms "conciliation caucus" and "shuttling in the context of a conciliation" are synonymous.

A conciliation caucus may or may not result in a written agreement between the parties which the parties may or may not sign in the presence of the other, although a notary is recommended in instances of this sort. In a conciliatory caucus an agreement may be reached that is not written down. A conciliation caucus may occur after a mediation has adjourned. A conciliation caucus may or may not result in a mediation. The conciliation caucus is distinguished by the physical absence of either or both parties. This absence has significant implications for neutrality and the complexity of communications.

A neutral third party who meets with only one party is subject to allegations that "behind-closed-door" deals are being made. This can occur with both mediation or conciliation caucuses.

The management of this concern must be done differently in the conciliation caucus. There are two basic variables to contend with: first, the origin of the conciliation process in the context of a mediation; second, the origin of the conciliation process without a mediative context. In the first instance, the conciliation process is initiated during the course of the mediation, when for practical reasons, i.e., the parties can no longer meet on a particular day and then cannot or will not meet physically again. In this instance, the mediator should have already introduced the possibility of the caucus to the parties as described above. Thus, any subsequent caucusing would have already been anticipated by the parties. Indeed, they may have requested the use of that process by their demand for separation or by their need to save time, money and the effort required to transport themselves to an agreed-upon location.

Where no mediation has occurred, the parties have not been formally introduced to the process before the process began. Consequently, the mediator/conciliator should do so. However, where in the introduction to the mediation, procedures and definitions have been more formally laid out, in conciliation the need for formality is often less significant since the parties are often engaged in a set of communications unilaterally initiated by the professional. The skills of suasion, clarity and non-personal approaches to evaluations are the most critical considerations, not the formality that is associated with a mediation hearing.

The reduced need for formality results partially from the relative ease occasioned by the absence of the adversaries. People seem more threatened, more "on-stage," when confronted with the persona of their foe. Using a very rigid structure to control exchanges in a tense situation is obviously not appropriate in the absense of the tension levels that triggered the use of formality initially. Consequently, the conciliation caucus can be introduced by saying, for example, "I will speak with the other party and get back to you." In this fashion, the disputant knows that you will be speaking to the other with permission to do so even though the conversation is private.

The concern for "equal time" does not normally arise in the conciliatory context. The party to whom you are not speaking is not waiting for you in the same fashion as during a mediation caucus. He may be going about his daily affairs as he otherwise would, and is in no position to know how much time you are spending with the other side.

Time continues to play an important role nonetheless. Having an on-going conflict fatigues people engaged in a conciliation caucus, although the intensities of the effort may not equal, in peak measures, those experienced while one is waiting outside a closed door. Yet the total volume of effort could very well be the same in mediation as in conciliation.

Money also continues to be an item of concern, and there appears to be no indication that greater lapses of time, measured not in minutes or hours of involvement, but total elapsed time in days, weeks or years, necessarily involve greater financial expenditures. The variances that arise can be taken into account by the mediator and placed in the appropriate categories of consideration.

If a choice is to be made between mediation caucusing and conciliation caucusing, several relevant factors must be considered: 1) the needs/wants of the parties singly and together; 2) the relative time/energy demands of both options in particular situations, and 3) which route is most likely to produce an accommodation. These are strongly linked.

In the course of a mediation, the mediator and/or the parties may become fatigued, or, as is more commonly believed, may simply "run out of time." Other commitments may interfere with continuance. At that point, there may be no need to meet again, perhaps because only details have yet to be resolved, or perhaps because of practical considerations. A conciliation caucus can result in time and money savings. Since mediation is a voluntary process, a consensually based decision needs to be made regarding the use of a conciliation caucus.

In some instances, a mediation caucus may use less time, money and energy. This possible advantage would derive from the opportunity for the clients to speak directly to one another, to examine documents and gather immediate responses. Elapsed time measured in days or weeks might be less, although hours actually spent in the process might be greater than in a conciliation caucus. Because the mediator can normally converse with only one of the parties at a time, communication is slower than in a mediation.

The greater the number of strategies one can bring to bear upon a conflict, the greater the likelihood that the conflict will be successfully resolved. This chapter outlined the options generated by caucusing. As a result, the mediator should have a clearer idea about using this technique.

Visualize conflicts in which you might utilize caucusing. How would you use this technique and when?

Note

1. Burgoon, Judee K. and Saine, Thomas; The Unspoken Dialogue—*An Introduction to Nonverbal Communication;* Houghton Mifflin Co., 1928, p. 54.

VII. A Mediation: The Most Complex Case

Introduction to Fact Synopsis

This is a simulated conflict which contains many of the issues which ordinarily attend conflicts involving intellectual properties, involving issues of patents and copyrights. The simulation demonstrates the process of mediation and the techniques used to arrive at settlement through accommodation. While the simulation is fictitious, it is an amalgam of different cases with similar issues.

It should be noted that all mediations require a minimum of one session which usually requires a maximum of three and one-half hours. Mediations involving such complex issues as those presented here would require a minimum of two sessions. Since some issues have purposely been left unresolved in the mediation and referred to arbitration, an additional session would be required to frame the submission for arbitration.

Please read the "fact synopsis" and then visualize the mediation session. You will note that the mediator relies heavily upon the use of questioning. He also uses the other processes which have been described earlier.

Fact Synopsis

Frank Johnston, a 62-year old man, has worked for 25 years as a basic plastics research chemist for a large oil company, Whitney Corporation of America. It has recently acquired ESP, a drug manufacturing division. Frank has developed a software program over several years in his evening hours that involves economic modeling for the marketing of proprietary drugs. He has the use of the computer at work, but has his own computer at home which uses a different language. A few months ago, Frank was not offered a promotion to head chemist, and has heard rumors about being laid off. He has three years to go before full retirement, and is very concerned because there has been some antagonism with his supervisor. He has no employment or invention agreement.

The drug division is in some financial difficulty and has discovered that a competing corporation has offered Frank payment and a percentage of the profits for his software. Whitney Corporation of America says that it owns the program and wants the rights to the program.

Frank's wife, Victoria, works for NARP (National Association of Retired Persons). Frank has hired Linda Smith as his attorney since she is a trusted friend of the family, even though she is not familiar with this type of litigation. NARP, therefore, has agreed to pay for the best trade secret lawyer in the country as co-counsel for Frank because they believe this case involves age discrimination.

Linda Smith has attempted to resolve this matter with John Roberts, Whitney Corporation of America's attorney, to no avail. She suggested the use of the Dispute Mediation Service of Dallas, a neutral third party, to facilitate settlement talks and has contacted Richard Evarts, the Executive Director. Both attorneys have full authority from the parties to negotiate a binding settlement.

SIMULATION—CONCILIATION

Conciliation: A Prelude to Mediation

Conciliation is the first stage of settlement. During this stage the mediator has two goals. The first goal is to schedule a mediation. The second is to discover grounds for accommodation. Seldom are parties simply willing to show up. They have questions that need to be answered regarding the process and the effect of mediation. They must also be persuaded that their opponent will participate in good faith and that there is some hope of settlement.

In striving to schedule a mediation or to discover grounds for accommodation the mediator/conciliator seeks to ask questions that require the client to assess the cost of not resolving the conflict and the benefits of attempting a speedy resolution. Great patience is required here. The client must arrive at his own conclusion at his own speed. The mediator must not attempt to coerce or "shame" the parties into participation. Participation under such circumstances is usually doomed, often encouraging the parties to sabotage the agreement at the last moment.

The mediator must permit the parties to visualize alternative futures and select the future that most closely conforms to their objectives. Given the skillful use of questioning, the participants usually conclude that mediation may well produce a less painful and expensive future and, therefore, is worth trying.

A mediation can only be scheduled if the mediator has successfully accomplished three preliminary tasks. First, the respondent must understand the process of mediation and have some grounds for believing that it might work. Obversely, he must also conclude that if the mediation does not succeed, he will not be worse off than before. Second, the respondent must believe that the initiator has a willingness to accommodate some of his needs. Third, both parties must have respect for and confidence in the mediator.

Scheduling a meeting requires a recognition that the responding party will probably "posture" and deny his availability for several of the suggested meeting times. The wise conciliator is always armed with alternative times, dates and places for the mediation session. Clarity of commitment in scheduling is vital. A letter confirming times, dates and locations (with a map of the location) should be sent to the parties on the day of setting. Telephone contact should be made with the clients the day before the meeting time as a reminder.

Discovering grounds for accommodation is a risky, but necessary, business. The mediator must probe just deeply enough to determine the positions of the parties. Probing too deeply will open up the whole case in an inappropriate environment. The environment is usually inappropriate for complex settlements because it usually consists of a telephone conversation with only one of the parties. The telephone provides insufficient non-verbal and visual clues regarding the real positions of the parties. It is far too easy to terminate the negotiating process by hanging up the telephone. Finally, it is very easy for the respondent to make demands before he has fully thought through his negotiating position and before he knows the real negotiating position of his opponent. Negotiating positions taken over the telephone tend to be extreme.

The discovery of the basic positions of the parties and some of the grounds for accommodation provides the mediator with enough information to simulate mentally the probable interplay between the parties and to identify possible scenarios for settlement. A well-prepared and well-informed mediator is ready to take effective control of the argument, quickly identify the negotiating distances between the parties and generate alternative solutions to the controversy. The prelude concludes with the mediator well prepared and the mediation date set. The symphony of settlement can now begin.

SIMULATION—MEDIATION

The Mediation Simulation and Settlement

A description of the dynamics of this particular mediation requires the reader to visualize all interchanges between the parties.

Several caveats are necessary. It is important to note that this simulation is designed as an illustration, not as an actual mediation. Complex conflicts usually require several sessions, often lasting three hours each. Secondly, the degree of affective involvement by the parties is limited because the respective counsel for each disputant has been empowered with full negotiating authority. The absence of the initiator (Mr. Frank Johnston) permits more rapid progress than might ordinarily occur. This assumes, of course, that the client would prefer, ordinarily, to be present during the session. Interpersonal dynamics always change when the speaker, whether attorney or client, has an audience. Finally, the conflict, if resolved, is usually resolved in its entirety. Therefore, the addition of an arbitration to resolve the specific money issues is something of a rarity. Nevertheless, the purpose of the simulation is to demonstrate the full range of alternative dispute resolution mechanisms. Obviously, arbitration is an important and viable, albeit less desirable alternative to consensus based decision making.

The simulation begins with the mediator introducing himself to both parties. Note that the mediator calls the parties by title (Mr. Roberts and Ms. Smith), not by their first names. This establishes a distance between the mediator and the clients, in what is otherwise a rather informal process. Next, the mediator sets the ground rules for the conduct of the session. These include the simple rules of courtesy and maintenance of decorum. The mediator asks each party if they consider him capable of maintaining neutrality and if they have known him in any other context. It is important here to maintain both the appearance and the reality of neutrality. The parties are also asked if they have read, understood and are now willing to sign the waiver and consent form. Unless this form is signed, the mediation cannot proceed. It insulates the mediator from subpoena and his records from subpoena *duces tecum*. In some instances it is necessary to devise a written declaration between the parties that pledges them not to use the mediation session as a means of discovery of facts that might be used in any subsequent lawsuit should the mediation fail. The parties are told that counsel for the initiator will speak first, setting forth her client's expectations. She is also requested to summarize what she believes to be the position of the Company. The purpose here is to gauge the degree of consonance between the reality and the vilification of the opposing position. The mediator also indicates that he will ask questions throughout the process to clarify the positions of the respective parties. Unilateral cross questioning between the parties is discouraged.

The mediation session then begins with a pledge from both parties to move conscientiously to a solution for a common problem.

During the presentation by the counsel for the initiator it becomes clear that three issues are central to the dispute. First, her client has injured feelings from a recent decision in which he was passed over for promotion. This "slight" has led him to contemplate revenge against his company by selling his economic modeling program to another company. Secondly, Johnston fears for his job security and is sensitive about his age, which he feels has been held against him in the decision regarding his possible promotion. Additionally, he now fears that he may be forced to leave the company before he is 65 years old and that his retirement income will be adversely affected by early departure.

Finally, Johnston feels that he has developed the program on his own time and wants to sell his program to the highest bidder. Note that the first two concerns are primarily affective. While solutions to these problems must take substantive form, the problems themselves are deeply emotional. The last concern, while substantively an issue of Johnston's ownership of the process and his right to sell it, is also an issue overlaid with feelings regarding independence and "rights" to do something with "his" property.

The position of the Company is based upon six concerns. First, the Company wants to obtain rights to utilize the process invented by Johnston. Secondly, the Company wants to prevent the process from falling into the hands of a competitor. Third, the Company wants to establish a precedent which will discourage attempts of its other employees to retain rights to products invented by them. Fourth, the Company wants to avoid unfavorable publicity which may emerge if an agreement is not reached. Fifth, the Company wants to minimize its costs in proceeding, realizing that litigation is not only expensive but time-consuming. Time might permit other inventors to devise a similar process or make the process itself obsolete. Finally, the Company wants to prevent Johnston's departure from its employment, realizing that he would take with him a considerable amount of information about the Company's operations, pending inventions and policies.

If the issues are arranged in the order of their presentation and examined for compatibility of interest between the parties, the grounds for accommodation are identified. The mediator will often note that the order of presentation is not necessarily indicative of the order of importance given to each expectation. Nevertheless, a measure of time invested in presenting each point and the number of adjectives used in describing each point will usually indicate the degree of importance attached to that point. The greater time investment and the more emotional the appeal, the higher the importance usually attached to that point.

The letter "C" after each issue indicates that this issue is compatible with a demand issued from the opposing side. The number of the issue with which compatibility is assumed has been listed next to each "C". The letter "I" indicates incompatibility between the positions. While the Company listed only six concerns, two additional concerns have been inferred by the mediator from the positions previously taken by the Company.

Company's Position	Johnston's Position	
1. obtain rights to process	1. sell rights	C-1
2. exclude competitor from process	2. job security	C-2
3. establish precedent	3. not an issue	C-3
4. avoid bad publicity	4. job security	C-4
5. minimize costs in proceeding	5. job security	C-5
6. prevent departure of employee	6. desire to stay through retirement	C-6
7. minimize costs of acquisition	7. maximize value of product	I-7
8. defuse Johnston's hostility	8. deal with feelings of no promotion	C-8

By listing the stated aims of the Company and Johnston, it is soon apparent that a consensus of interest lies hidden beneath the emotional hostility of the parties. Johnston wants to sell his rights and the Company wants to obtain them. True, the Company might be able to obtain them through legal action. But such legal action would be time-consuming and might drive Johnston into the opposing camp. It might also permit competitors the opportunity to replicate the system, or even improve upon it before the process could be utilized.

The Company might desire a precedent to discourage similar actions by its employees. But would a battle with Johnston establish that precedent? How long would it take? What is the comparative value of the precedent vis-a-vis utilization of the process? Might the Company find another way, such as a detailed employment contract, to protect its future interests? Since Johnston is not really concerned with this issue, would it be possible to gain his future cooperation and allow the past disagreement to pass away?

The Company desires to avoid bad publicity, minimize its costs in proceeding and prevent utilization of the process by a competitor. If Johnston is still part of the Company, his interest would be served by its increased profitability; a profitability most easily achieved by reducing costs and increasing revenues. This same process of reasoning applies to the need for the Company to defuse Johnston's hostility and for his need to address his feelings of slight over the issue of promotion. If both the Company and Johnston resolve this issue, then both parties will be more effective contributors to the prosperity that each desires.

If these issues can be examined rationally, both sides will discover the degree of compatibility that exists between them. Since they have not been able to attain that discovery, it falls to the mediator to clarify the parties' perceptions of their mutual interest. In doing so, he will focus upon the one remaining issue that divides the parties: the manner and amount of payment for the process.

For the benefit of this demonstration of alternative processes of conflict resolution, the issue of the manner and amount of payment has been left for resolution through arbitration.

THE ARBITRATION—SIMULATION AND SETTLEMENT

Advance agreement to resolve issues through mediation may include provision to arbitrate any issues that were not resolved in the mediation session. Arbitration might be defined as the intervention of a neutral third party(s), who, intervening at the request of the parties, is empowered by the parties with the right to settle the matters of controversy submitted to him through the issuance of an arbitration award. Arbitration is often viewed as a private court. Unlike legal proceedings, however, arbitration is usually far less formal and does not strictly apply the rules of evidence.

The initiation of arbitration proceedings usually occurs on the basis of a "demand for arbitration" or a "submission to arbitration." A demand usually invokes an arbitration clause already contained in an existing contract between the parties. A submission to arbitration is a consensual document which sets forth the matter to be arbitrated. It often carefully identifies the range within which the award may be issued. For example, it might state that the award will call for not less than "x" nor more than "y" in payment to one party. The submission might also state the standards of decision which must be applied to the instant case. An excellent source book on arbitration is *How Arbitration Works,* by Elkouri, *op cit.*

Arbitration is a well established and well regarded process. Many commercial contracts contain arbitration clauses within them as a means of resolving disputes expeditiously. Elkouri even cites the last will and testament of George Washington as containing an arbitration clause. Yet, its binding nature demands special precautions. Great care must be exercised in selecting the arbitrator and in deciding whether an expert or a generalist is preferable. Further, the submission should be as explicit as the parties will permit. Finally, the arguments should be cogent, well reasoned and easily understood by the arbitrator.

In a real arbitration, counsel for both parties would present their respective arguments and supporting documents if any. They may also present witnesses who might describe current practices in the particular topic of dispute. At the conclusion of the hearing, the arbitrator closes the session (most arbitrations are completed within one day) and retires to write the award. The award is usually produced within ten to forty-five days of the session and, if unchallenged, is binding upon the parties. Challenges to arbitration awards are onerous and infrequently successful.

In this particular simulation, the parties presented the arbitrator with the task of deciding the issues of "damages, royalty interests, ownership and compensation due the parties in regard to the development, production and use of (a) software package" which Johnston invented. The arbitrator awarded $50,000 to be paid to Johnston and a 5% interest in the gross revenues produced by the software package for 15 years. In conducting the hearing and in making his final award the arbitrator followed the Commercial Arbitration Rules of the American Arbitration Association. The arbitrator was required only to determine the financial compensation to be paid to the inventor since the parties had already agreed to permit the Whitney Corporation to utilize the program. In a real sense, the mediation agreement partially framed the range of decision within which the arbitrator had to operate.

VIII. Case Studies

In this chapter, three case studies will be made. The first will deal with a relatively simple problem between a landlord and a tenant. Secondly, we will discuss a more intricate conflict between an employer and his ex-employee. Lastly, we will review a dispute between a divorced couple over visitation and child-support payments. Each study is based upon a case actually done by one or more of the authors. The facts in the stories and the agreements reached have been altered to assure the privacy of the parties and are not intended to qualify as interpretations of what has been said. The names have been changed to protect the parties involved.

As you read these studies, you will probably ask yourself several questions about specific techniques used. In some locations, the narrative will provide good clues about how specific outcomes were actually reached. However, the studies are not transcriptions of dialogues, so that inevitably some details of the transaction will be missing.

Case Study #1: Ima Shore and Swaying Oak Apartments

Ms. Ima Shore leased a two-bedroom apartment at Swaying Oak Apartments. In exchange for a rental reduction of $50.00 per month and a month-to-month lease, she agreed to assist the manager with apartment cleaning and some bookkeeping assignments. After four months of this arrangement, the manager, Allen Vane, decided that Ms. Shore's services were not worth paying for. He also decided that since bad feelings existed and would likely increase when she was notified that her services were no longer needed, he would demand that she leave.

Ms. Shore refused to leave without her deposit in hand, as she did not trust Mr. Vane to return it. She was referred to a mediator. The mediator discovered that Ms. Shore needed the deposit money in order to secure a lease on another apartment. He also learned from Mr. Vane that he was willing to return the deposit provided Ms. Shore was out of the apartment by the deadline. At first, Mr. Vane resisted returning the deposit before Ms. Shore moved, but then offered to return 50% of the deposit at the beginning of the move, and the rest the moment she had completed moving. Ms. Shore agreed to the compromise solution.

The parties attested to a document similar to this one:

Witness this agreement made this 18th day of August, 1982 between Ima Shore, currently residing at 1813 Cracked Oak Lane, #13, and Swaying Oak Apartments.

The parties agree to the following terms and conditions:

1. Ima Shore will commence removing her belongings from 1813 Cracked Oak Lane, #13 on August 19, 1982, at 6:00 pm.

2. When Ima Shore has removed her piano and Sony television set from the aforementioned apartment, and placed them in a rented vehicle, the representative for Swaying Oak Apartments will give her a company check in the amount of $150.00, which amount is 50% of the security deposit paid by Ima Shore to Swaying Oak Apartments on March 15, 1982.

3. Ms. Ima Shore may immediately seek to cash the check given to her. If the check does not clear because of insufficient funds, because a stop-payment has been placed on the check, or for any other restriction imposed by Swaying Oak Apartments, Ms. Shore may return her items to the aforementioned apartment, and will arrange additional mediation of the issues. In this event, Swaying Oak Apartment agrees to pay up to $50.00 for the rental of the truck unless some negligent or intentionally destructive act is undertaken by Ms. Shore or any of her relatives or friends against the property or person of Swaying Oak Apartments and/or its employees.

4. When Ima Shore has completed removing her remaining possessions and appropriately cleaned the premises (as required by the cleaning agreement attached), the representatives of Swaying Oak Apartments will give to Ms. Ima Shore a company check in the amount of $150.00 provided the unit has been cleaned according to the terms of the lease which originally governed the tenancy of Ms. Shore. Upon her vacating the premises, Ms. Ima Shore and the representative of Swaying Oak Apartments will inspect the apartment and check off and sign a list provided by Swaying Oak Apartments describing its condition.

5. This final check of $150.00, when honored by the bank against whose funds it is drawn, will constitute a complete and final payment of all funds owed to Ms. Ima Shore by Swaying Oak Apartments. If subsequent damages to the apartment are discovered that have not been checked "satisfactory" or otherwise approved by both parties to this agreement, then both parties will seek settlement of the differences through mediation.

THE PARTIES TO THIS AGREEMENT FULLY UNDERSTAND IT AND ACKNOWLEDGE THAT THIS AGREEMENT IS THE FINAL SETTLEMENT OF THE DISPUTE BETWEEN THEM OVER THE MATTERS MENTIONED IN THE AGREEMENT. THEY INTEND FOR THE AGREEMENT TO BE ENFORCEABLE ACCORDING TO ITS TERMS IN ANY COURT OF COMPETENT JURISDICTION.

Case Study #2:

Gene Tight, a construction engineer, was hired by his close personal friend, S. L. Ander, to manage Over-Run Excavating Company. The job required a significant amount of local travel. Mr. Tight was to travel to construction sites in his Toyota, a circumstance that both Tight and Ander recognized as undesirable.

To restructure the situation, they agreed that Ander would purchase the Toyota from Tight for the amount Tight owed on the vehicle. Tight's motive for this derived from his financial circumstances and his belief that the vehicle was worth no more than what was owed on it at the time the arrangement was made (May 17, 1981).

Further, the parties agreed that Tight would purchase a pick-up truck which would be financed by Ander. The payments would be withdrawn from Tight's paycheck on a weekly basis.

The deal was struck as the parties later confirmed, and all went well. In fact, business improved and Ander decided to forgive the loan on the truck. This was accomplished by ceasing withholding of the weekly truck payment. Tight later argued that the offer was a bonus and that the truck became his, free and clear of all liens. No title exchange occurred. Ander counterclaimed that the offer was for a salary raise in the amount equivalent to the weekly truck payment.

All went well, however, until either the general business climate deteriorated (Ander's version) or management made poor decisions (Tight's version). Tight was either fired or resigned (again, according to which party was speaking). Tight sought the title for the truck and was told that he owed $1,800 on the vehicle.

The mediator noted that the reason for the separation of the parties had to be fractionated from the issue of the control of the vehicle. Both parties agreed to refrain from mentioning the issues surrounding the separation. Then the mediator proceeded to discover the needs of the parties. The primary need for both parties seemed to be to save face. The mediator sought to accomplish this by subtly reassuring both of their professional competence, their great ability to refrain from all-out assaults upon their foe, and the like, without engaging in comparisons between the two. The secondary need was hidden behind a stated desire that each make money on the exchange, which turned out to be a face-saving tactic. The secondary need was to minimize losses.

The mediator sought to help the parties discover all the ways of resolving the situation. A trade of the vehicles was rejected by Ander, who argued that he had made over $2,000 in payments, leaving the vehicle with a net worth of about $600, adding that he had no use for a pick-up truck. Mr. Tight countered with an offer of $600 for the Toyota, which was rebuffed. Then, in caucus, the mediator discovered that Tight would be willing to sell the pick-up if Ander would have the truck painted, which could be done readily at one of the Company's shops.

Meeting with S. L. Ander, the mediator found that this arrangement would be acceptable. In joint session, the parties then began to haggle on the price. The parties agreed that the vehicle would not demand $1,800. Tight suggested $900. Ander said that any fool could get $1,200 if the vehicle was painted. Warning against insult, the mediator then asked about payments on the vehicle. Ander said that one payment was late and others were due, but should not be subtracted from the selling price if that was less than the amount owed. Mr. Tight argued that the payments should be subtracted from the selling price, as was customary, and the balance should reflect the $600 in parts he bought to repair the vehicle and at least $300 (down from the $1000 he felt was reasonable for repairs he had done himself). After several sessions, the parties came to the following settlement. "Party 1" refers to Gene Tight and "Party 2" to S. L. Ander.

The Agreement

1. Party 1 will attempt to sell a 1978 Dodge pickup truck, VIN #400012, for the amount of $1000 immediately after the truck is painted. Net proceeds from the sale of the vehicle exceeding $1000 will be split evenly between the parties. Net proceeds will be calculated on the basis of the sale price, as documented by a signed bill of sale, less the costs of advertising the vehicle. The costs will be limited to newspaper advertising.

2. Party 2 will paint the 1978 Dodge pickup truck at his own cost, including materials and labor. The painting will be complete by February 18, 1982, at 6:00 pm, or five days after Party 1 delivers the truck to Party 2, whichever is later.

3. Party 2 will purchase from Party 1 a 1981 Toyota Celica VIN #123456, for the amount owed by Party 1 to Joe's Easy Finance Credit Union on Loan #888-04. This purchase will take place by the tenth day after the sale of the pickup truck referred to in Clause 1 above to any third party or to Party 1. The sales price will be determined by the payoff on the loan at the time of purchase.

4. On the 28th day of February, 1982, Party 1 will pay Party 2 $50.00. This sum will reduce the total price as mentioned in Clause 6 below. A payment made five days or more after the due date will be considered late. A late charge of $5.00 will be paid in that instance. The postmark will be used to determine the date of receipt, unless the payment is hand-delivered, in which case a cash receipt will provide proof of payment date.

5. Party 1 will act as salesman for the pickup truck. The final sale of the vehicle requires the approval of Party 2. This approval is made contingent only upon the receipt by Party 2 of $1000 in cash or certified funds. No other conditions are made.

6. On March 28, 1982, Party 1 will begin paying to Party 2 the sum of $100.00 per month as a truck payment for the pickup identified above if and only if the truck is not sold by then. Party 1 will pay Party 2 the sum of $1125 commencing on March 28. The total of $1125 includes the reduction mentioned in Clause 5 above. Other conditions for payment remain as mentioned above.

Payments will be made in 11 consecutive monthly installments of $100.00, commencing on March 28, 1982. The due date is the 28th day of each month. The last payment of $25.00 will be paid on February 28, 1983. Upon receipt of the final payment, Party 2 will sign the title and other appropriate documents to transfer ownership to Party 1.

7. Failure to make payments can result in the repossession of either vehicle by the financing agent. Party 1 is financing the Toyota and Party 2 is financing the pickup. The intent to repossess must be made in writing via certified mail, return receipt requested, and must be mailed at least ten days prior to repossession. Failure to acknowledge the mailed notice does not obviate the repossessor's rights to confiscate. Any attempt to make a vehicle unavailable for repossession will make the withholding party liable for the costs of repossession (including wrecker service and reasonable mediator or attorney fees), plus $500.00. Both parties will inform the other upon oral or written request of the whereabouts of the vehicle, and will take due care to protect the vehicle from damage and/or theft. Each party will insure the vehicle as required by Texas state law.

8. Severence pay in the amount of $660.00 is to be paid by Party 2 to Party 1 upon the sale of the truck to a third party, or the completion of payments by Party 1.

THE PARTIES TO THIS AGREEMENT FULLY UNDERSTAND IT AND ACKNOWLEDGE THAT THIS AGREEMENT IS THE FINAL SETTLEMENT OF THE DISPUTE BETWEEN THEM OVER THE MATTERS MENTIONED HEREIN. HOWEVER, IN THE EVENT OF LITIGATION, THE PARTIES AGREE THAT THIS DOCUMENT AND THE UNDERSTANDING ARISING FROM IT DO NOT AFFECT ANY PRIOR AGREEMENT ENTERED INTO, NOR DOES THIS UNDERSTANDING REFLECT ANY INTENT OF THE PARTIES EXCEPT AS RELATED TO THE TERMS EXPRESSED HEREIN. FURTHER, THE PARTIES AGREE THAT SHOULD ANY DISPUTE ARISE OUT OF THE PERFORMANCE OR INTERPRETATION OF THIS AGREEMENT, THEY WILL APPEAR, EACH AT THE REQUEST OF THE OTHER PARTY, FOR AN ADDITIONAL MEDIATION SESSION, BEFORE SEEKING JUDICIAL REVIEW.

Case Study #3:

The following example involves an issue of visitation and child support. Jane Van Jones is the new wife of John Van Jones. William Van Jones is an 11-year old who is the natural son of John Van Jones and Mildred Stone. William lives with Jane and John in Denver, while Mildred, John's former wife and the natural mother of William, lives in Amarillo, Texas.

The adults began to quarrel after Mildred stopped making child support payments, yet insisted upon seeing the child, who had been awarded to the custody of John in an uncontested divorce. Mildred was angered by John's marriage to Jane a year prior to the suspension of her support payments. Mildred claimed that she was being denied adequate visitation with the child, noting that on some occasions when she traveled to Denver, she was denied visitation because of what she described as "lame excuses." She came to believe that Jane did not want to share William and John out of a fear that the old loves would return.

Jane denied any such claim, arguing that Mildred came unannounced to visit William and on two occasions, William was committed to other activities. She claimed that Mildred was just jealous that John had found a new (and perhaps better) woman who didn't have other men in her life. By trading such insinuations, the adults became involved in a series of confrontations.

After a year and a half of delayed hearings and several thousand dollars in attorneys' fees, the parties' time, energy and financial resources became seriously depleted, and they decided to settle their issues through mediation.

The meeting began with a great deal of tension expressed in the non-verbal communication of the parties, in part due to a confrontation over the mediation site. The unavailability of mediation services in Mildred's hometown was used by the mediator as a dead-lock breaker.

The major initial barrier resulted from the insinuations of jealousy by Jane and Mildred. The mediator chose to work around this issue by asking the parties what benefit was to be gained by pursuing it.

"I know she was jealous," said Jane.

"How did you know that?"

"It was obvious by the way she glared at me."

"So, do you know that she glared at you, or do you know that she was jealous?"

"It just seemed obvious. Besides, she said that I had better not stand in her way of her seeing her child and her husband."

"That's not what I said," Mildred interrupted. "I just told her that she better let me see William, and John, too, if he wanted. After all, John and I are still friends!"

After a few more interchanges along these lines, the mediator said,

"What will be gained by knowing who is and is not jealous?"

"Nothing," said John. "Just more fighting."

"No," said Jane, "We'll just keep upsetting William."

"Well, are we ready to put this behind us? I know that everyone has some hurt feelings. Will those feelings be better dealt with by talking about how to arrange visitation and child support?"

With the agreement of the parties to engage in a dialogue about the specifics of visitation and support payments, the mediator had accomplished a major feat.

Deadlocks occurred at several other points in this process. The first deadlock developed over when to initiate the summer visitation William was to have with Mildred. Mildred wanted William to begin his visits with her immediately after his school term ended. John and Jane objected, arguing that if Mildred wanted the child until September, no time would be allowed for the Joneses to vacation together as a unit. The Joneses stated that mid-July would be the best time for visitation to commence, since they would then have six weeks in which to take a family vacation. They said that they needed six weeks to have adequate flexibility for John and Jane's employers, who could not always guarantee that employees could take vacations during their first choice of time periods. Mildred countered by noting that the child spent most of his time with the Joneses and that the child's natural mother had a right to spend time with the child. The mediator asked Mildred how much time she needed to have her rights respected. She reasserted that three months was necessary. Did the child's opinion matter to her? Yes, it did.

The mediator was given a copy of a letter from William to Mildred stating that he would like to spend a portion of the summer with both parents. After the letter was read aloud, Mildred was asked if she had any quarrel with it, and she said she did not. The mediator asked if July 1 would be an acceptable starting date for the summer visitation. After some haggling, the parties agreed to that date.

The other major point of contention concerned the payment of child support. Mildred stated that she could no longer afford the $250.00 monthly payments, pointing out that her income had fallen, while that of the Joneses had risen. She offered to pay $200.00 per month. The Joneses acknowledged that their income had risen, but argued that their expenses had also risen. They requested that support payments missed be repaid and that if that was done, they would agree to $200.00 per month. The unpaid amount was $2,500. Mildred stated she had spent $500 on legal fees. She offered the $2,000 remaining. Although the parties haggled for a considerable period of time, they eventually settled at $2,000.

MEMORANDUM OF AGREEMENT

This is a memorandum of agreement between John Van Jones, Jane Van Jones and Mildred Stone. William Van Jones and Mildred Stone are the natural parents of William Van Jones, born April 28, 1974. Jane Van Jones is the wife of John Van Jones. The Van Joneses are currently residents of Denver, Colorado, and Mildred Stone is a resident of Amarillo, Texas.

The memorandum of agreement states the intentions of the parties regarding the periods of visitation which shall occur between William Van Jones, a child, and Mildred Stone, his natural mother. This memorandum forms the basis of a working agreement between the parties, which shall be reduced to proper motion by the attorneys of the respective parties.

BACKGROUND: This memorandum of agreement has emerged from discussion held between the parties with the assistance of a mediator. These discussions began on April 17, 1981, and have extended to the date of this agreement. All discussions have been premised on the best interests of the child and on the conscientious intentions of all parties to reach an agreement based in equity and consensus.

Specifics on Visitation between William and Mildred Stone and times for return to the Jones household, 1982–1983:

1. William would visit Mildred Stone from July 1, 1981 to September 1, 1981.

2. William would visit with Mildred Stone during the Widget Makers Conference currently planned by the Mediocre Middle School in Denver, Colorado, where William is currently enrolled.

3. William would visit Mildred Stone during Christmas, 1981, from December 22, 1981 to January 2, 1982.

4. William would visit with Mildred Stone during the spring vacation period currently offered by the Middle School except that if William requested this period for a family vacation and the Van Joneses agree, this period would be traded and the same number of days added to the period of visitation with Mildred Stone during the summer. Mildred Stone agrees to give special consideration to such a request from William, and, except in extraordinary circumstances, to grant such a request.

5. William would visit with Mildred Stone for a period of four days each fall, alternating the fall Parent-Teacher Conferences with Thanksgiving vacation. In the fall of 1981, William will visit Mildred Stone during the Parent-Teacher Conference.

6. William would remain with the Van Joneses at least eight days every Christmas holiday period. Visits with Mildred Stone shall be arranged on a yearly basis between the parties, and every other year, William will spend Christmas and New Year's Day with Mildred Stone.

7. During all other periods, the Van Jones will exercise custody of William, with all the rights, privileges and responsibilities pertaining thereto.

OTHER QUESTIONS OF VISITATION

1. The entire concept of visiting is based upon a sense of mutual trust and respect.

2. The necessity of flexibility between the parties may require certain modifications to the pattern of visitation that shall be the topic of negotiation held in that climate of mutual trust and respect.

3. Periodic trips to Denver by Mildred Stone with five days' notice to the Van Joneses, will permit local visitation, which shall be in addition to other visitation periods except in the case of an emergency in the immediate family, in which requirement of notice is waived.

4. Opportunities for William may arise in the future which will give all parents an opportunity to work together for his best interest by amending the rigid structures of visitation. It is the intention of the parties to create such a climate.

EXPENSES

1. Mildred Stone agrees to pay all costs of transportation for William during his visits with her. Mildred Stone will choose the means of transportation. The Joneses agree to place William on the requested transportation and to cover the costs of getting William to the point of departure.

2. Special expenses of William may become the topic of future discussion between the parties in the spirit of cooperation already mentioned.

SUPPORT FOR THE CHILD

1. It is agreed that Mildred Stone will pay to the Van Joneses the sum of $200.00 per month on the first day of every month to help support the child.

2. On or before May 1, 1981, Mildred Stone will pay to the Van Joneses the sum of $2,000, an amount which covers in full all child support payments not paid to the Van Joneses.

EXECUTION OF THE AGREEMENT

1. It is agreed that the parties to this agreement will review it and return it with any suggestions for amendment, additions or deletions within ten days of this date.

2. It is also agreed that when the final form of the memorandum has been completed, which shall be before the Mediocre Middle School has its first fall break, it will be reduced to motion by the attorneys of the respective parties and entered in the court records.

FURTHER NEGOTIATION

Should any dispute arise out of the contents or execution of this agreement, the parties agree to return first to the Mediation Service in a conscientious attempt to resolve their differences. Further, the parties agree to continue negotiation until this agreement finds final form.

Signature of the parties:

A Final Note

The mediator was concerned that in the event of litigation, either party might jeopardize his rights when his intention at the time of the original agreement was called into account. Therefore, the mediator hoped to protect the parties by the above boiler-plate clause.

WHAT IS AN AGREEMENT?

The goal of all conflict management is the construction of agreements based in consensus. An agreement must be clear and specific, to permit the parties to perform under the terms of the agreement.

Agreements

The terms "agreement," "settlement," and "contract" are often used synonymously. Yet, definitional clarity produces a more precise understanding of the process of conflict management. An agreement may be defined as a definite, specific and concrete understanding between conflicting parties which sets forth the mutual expectations of the parties regarding performance of specific acts. The performance of these acts resolves a specific set of differences between the parties.

Note that in the definition of agreement, the document of resolution rests in a clear and unambiguous understanding of the *mutual* expectations of the parties. Without mutuality, no real agreement has been reached. Such "agreements" are sometimes called unilateral agreements. It is one of the premises of this book that unilateral agreements are not really agreements at all since they do not rest in consensus and demand performance from only one side. The mutuality of performance is one key element in agreement formulation. Another requirement of agreements is that specific acts of performance are required. These acts are symbolic vehicles of settlement without which the conflict would continue. The symbols of settlement differ across cultures. In the Western world money often constitutes the principal symbol of settlement. In other cultures, symbols may include elaborate ceremonies or acts of obeisance. Finally, agreements require a perception that the agreement is binding on both parties and that both parties intend to perform under its terms.

Ordinarily, agreements are issue oriented. Therefore, they often settle only parts of the controversy. Additionally, their consensual nature requires rapid performance often undemanded by the court. Because of these attributes, agreements rarely require enforcement in the courts.

Settlements

A much more difficult resolution might be termed a settlement. Settlement here is defined as a definitive, binding, consensual and encompassing resolution of all matters at dispute between contending parties.

Again, settlements have all of the attributes of agreements except that they strive to settle all issues, including affective and emotional issues. Therefore, some agreements will include provisions for statements of regret, apology or other items of feeling. Settlements are the broadest possible resolution. Since so much of what we suppose to be substance is actually affect in the minds of the parties, the broader the settlement the more affective it will appear. Nevertheless, all substantive issues must also be addressed to forge a settlement of fact as well as principle.

Settlements are also true meetings of the minds of the conflicting parties. Therefore, enforcement of a settlement is unnecessary. Here, the parties simply go about their performance without coercion or demand. Since they authored the document without force and invested it with their support, the vast majority of settlements find performance.

Contracts

A contract, as contrasted to settlements and agreements, might be defined as a promissory agreement between two or more persons that creates, modifies or destroys a relationship (Buffalo Pressed Steel Company v. Kirwan, 138 Md. 60, 113 A.)

This legalist definition of contracts emphasizes that people are involved in the agreement (the law extends this designation to corporations), that a relationship exists between the parties and that the document has created that relationship, modified it or destroyed it.

The structure of contracts requires that the contract answers the following questions entwined within the conflict:

1. who are the parties
2. what is the relationship, what is the performance
3. when did the relationship begin and end
4. where will performance occur
5. how will performance occur
6. how much (or what) will be paid for the performance
7. what if performance does not occur.

This same general structure is required of all agreements and settlements.

Common Elements

Elements that are common to settlements, agreements and contracts include: specificity of performance, clarity of terms and parties, mutuality of involvement and the consensual nature of the settlement.

Ideally, all forms of resolution should have the following characteristics:

1. written in clear terms
2. statement indicating the identity of the parties
3. statement of the relationship between the parties
4. summary of the conflict being settled by the agreement
5. terms of performance between the parties.
6. time of the agreement
7. time of the performance
8. an exchange of consideration between the parties.
9. a copy of the agreement given in its same form to both parties.
10. a statement of recourse if the agreement is not performed.
11. signature of the parties
12. witnesses to the signatures

Other Considerations

The simply analogy of a baseball game is useful: no hits, no runs, no errors, no one left on base, no spectator involvement and next year's schedule clearly established.

No hits means that no viable agreement can be coercive and require performance that the parties can not accomplish or that are illegal under commonly agreed upon elements of equity and the demands of the law.

No runs means that no one can be permitted to obtain all of the advantages without equal consideration for the other parties. Agreements must be conscionable. They must not establish inequities, but must create an equitable balance between the parties.

No errors means that agreements must not contain tangible errors of fact or errors of form that distort the names or identities of the parties. For example, an agreement for the distribution of marital property in a dissolution of marriage case can not exclude some items of property that one party "forgot to mention."

No spectator involvement means that third-parties not present or involved in the formulation of the agreement must not and can not be bound to the agreement.

No one left on base means that all parties involved in the controversy must be involved in the agreement and in the process used to arrive at the agreement.

Next year's schedule means that the parties must know how and when to perform under the agreement and must know what to do if performance does not occur. Here, the mediator or negotiator might wish to suggest the inclusion of a mediation clause which would establish a moral, and perhaps a legal commitment to return to the negotiation table should performance fail to occur to the satisfaction of both parties.

Conclusion

Three different types of resolution have been described. The most difficult form of resolution is called a settlement. The most common form of settlement is an agreement. The most frequently misused term of resolution is a contract. Not all agreements are contracts, but all true contracts contain agreements. Ironically, true agreements do not require enforcement and, therefore, need not be contracts. Unfortunately, many contracts are so imprecisely forged that they do not contain real agreements and, therefore, require enforcement.

IX. Introduction to the Ethics of Mediation

You are assigned a case involving two neighbors. There are charges and countercharges of harassment. You converse with both parties and discover that one is extremely meek and the other is aggressive. Given your concerns about neutrality you are afraid that the mediation might be damaged if you act to empower the former. On the other hand, you are afraid that if you fail to do so, you cannot feel assured that the outcome will be equitable. What *should* you do?

You are assigned another case. A husband and wife are arguing over the division of property. You have made some progress towards settlement when tempers flare. You call a caucus. One of the parties confesses to have been lying. This is threatening the potential success of the mediation. What *should* you do?

In a third case to which you have been assigned, a landlord is charging the tenant with sexual harassment, while the latter has countercharged that the landlord has stolen some articles. In caucus, both parties reveal that the charges are true. *Should* you turn this information over to authorities?

Many people have attempted to answer questions like these in many different contexts. They raise moral issues, the appropriate answers to which are as elusive as any that can be asked. The answers we give have a profound impact on human relations, for they bring forth fundamental attitudes towards self and society.

In the past, philosophers have answered moral questions in many ways. We shall discuss two predominant systems.[1] Following a discussion of moral questions, we shall discuss the ways in which law and morality interact. This will improve your understanding of the relationship between mediation and the law. This knowledge is important to the consideration of ethical problems in mediation.

Deontological Theories

Should we make moral decisions based upon the *consequences* of action, or should we ignore consequences because an act is right or wrong regardless of the consequences? Those who affirm the overriding importance of consequences can be called 'teleological moralists.' Those who deny this position can be called deontologists, which indicates their interest in the science of obligation.

Examine the first conflict. Let us say that you determine that it is wrong for your concern about the outcome to affect how you handle the situation. Perhaps you think there is something about mediation which makes the act of empowering undesirable in and of itself. Regardless of the consequences, you think that one should not "hinder" the process of mediation. Therefore, you decide that one should not act simply to insure that the outcome is equitable.

Your opinion is not based on what you believe the consequences might be but rather upon what was right in and of itself. You have committed yourself to a principle which does not vary according to differences in consequences. You are a deontological thinker.

Once you have arrived at this point, there is another kind of problem to be solved. Are there moral standards which do not vary from situation to situation, or must one evaluate each situation individually? If you take the former stance, then your position can be called *rule* deontological while the latter position can be termed *act* deontological. Dealing with the problem of situation versus uniformity has a lot to do with whether or not there can be rules to govern the acts of mediators, or whether a system of individualized evaluation must be created.

Once having solved this problem, you may ask, "How do you know if a rule applies in a given situation or that one circumstance demands a particular moral action?" Philosophers have been divided along two basic lines in answering questions like these. Some have held that reason is the proper basis for decision making, while some have argued that some form of intuition is preferable. Others have argued for some combination of reason and intuition. Or it may be that humans can decide to be rational or intuitional as they wish. If this were so, it would be impossible to base a system of knowledge on any single structure of human characteristics. Solving this problem is complex, and will have to be approached elsewhere.

Teleological Theories

In the second conflict, involving the division of property, the husband or wife (or both!) admit to having lied. Do you reveal this confession in order to manipulate the parties into coming to an agreement? Let us say that you determine that the consequences of the act are undesirable. A teleologist might ask what it is about an act that makes it right or wrong if it is not the consequences of that act. How is it possible, it might be asked, to know if an act is desirable if consequences are unobservable? They would conclude that the knowledge of the meaning of the act cannot be determined except by reference to consequences. Thus consequences are the basis upon which to judge the quality of an act.

Like deontologists, teleologists face the choice between constructing rules that cover all or certain given situations, or analyzing each situation on its own merits. Suppose you think that one must not reveal that Party A has lied since, on the whole, the consequences would be desirable (i.e. mediation would remain a possibility). You think that this conclusion might not hold in other circumstances since no other situation might be quite like this one. Your position could be called *act* teleological. If, on the other hand, you decide that you should not reveal the lie because the consequences for doing so are always, or almost always undesirable, your position could be called *rule* teleological.

Law and Morality

Finally we can consider the last simple situation. Here, the parties have admitted to violating the law. *Should* you notify the proper authorities? This question raises the issue of the proper relationship between law and morality (i.e. is it moral to report activities to the police?) and mediation and the law (i.e. which takes precedence?). The latter question will be discussed in the next section.

In answering these questions, it is necessary to make ethical inquiries. We may ask, for example, whether there is something intrinsic to the law and its subjects which requires reporting under some circumstance 'x'. This type of inquiry has already been briefly examined. It seems useful, instead, to allow the discussion to take a more political tone.

Why, you may ask, should politics be considered in a discussion of mediation? Most people have some understanding of what is political about the law. For example, legislators write laws and legislators are chosen through a process easily recognized as political. But what, exactly, is political about law-making? One could readily respond that what is political about law-making is the assertion of the community's interest in establishing standards of behavior. Here the political nature of the mediation process becomes apparent, for both in mediation and the law the community has a stake in the outcome. Mediation is different from the practice of law. Nonetheless, the issues of mediation are the norms of behavior over which there is conflict. Since both mediation and the law share a subject matter (although they may not share many similarities in process) and since the legal approach is a political one, then mediation is political.

It seems obvious that one can ask *moral* questions about *political* events. We must do so in order to make further inquiry into the politics of mediation possible. We want to ask, for example, "Should the mediator have absolute control over the mediation? Should the state require the mediation of disputes? Should mediation be financed through tax revenues? Should mediators report back to referral sources?"

Various political philosophies provide different answers to questions like these. The first of these questions is the broadest, so it will be used as a reference through which to explain the alternative political philosophies available to us.

If you hold that the state has the absolute right of intervention, then your political philosophy can be called 'absolutist' or 'totalitarian.' This philosophy involves the absolute denial of individual liberty and the absolute affirmation of the rights of the community.[2] Under a totalitarian regime, mediation would be possible by giving the mediator considerable power to control the meeting, set the agenda, etc. Some would assert that this cannot be called mediation.

On the other end of the scale is the belief that the community has no right of intervention whatsoever. The parties to the dispute, not the community (state), have the right to determine the outcome, the procedures, etc. The mediator's role is determined also, although the mediator as an individual would have certain rights, too. This belief can be called anarchism. Of course, you need not be an anarchist if you conceive of mediation as it was just described. An anarchist holds the principle of non-intervention to be true under all (or almost all) circumstances.

There are many alternatives to totalitarianism and anarchism. For want of space these will not be fully explored here. Instead, a brief description of some major alternatives will be given:[3]

> *Conflict principle*—it is morally permissible to intervene if one person's rights conflict with those of another.
> *Private harm principle*—intervention is allowable if so doing prevents harm to others.
> *Public Harm Principle*—Intervention is allowable to prevent harm to institutional practices that are in the public interest.
> *Legal paternalism*—intervention is allowable to prevent harm to the individual.
> *Extreme paternalism*—intervention is allowable to benefit the individual.
> *Welfare principle*—intervention is allowable if it benefits others.
> *Weak legal paternalism*—intervention is allowable to prevent harm to the individual if the risk of harm is extreme or not fully voluntary or if the intervention is necessary to determine the nature of the dangers involved.
> *Offense principle*—intervention is allowable to prevent some from offending others.
> *Legal moralism*—intervention is allowable if it is necessary to enforce society's view of morality.

One could use any of these principles, singly or in combination, in lieu of or in addition to the totalitarian or anarchistic principles to deny or assert the rights of the mediator and/or either of the disputants.

In mediation, conflicts over disputed rights are perhaps core considerations. The initiator may assert rights, as may the respondent, the mediator and the community. The mediator has to make many decisions to define the process which will be used to solve the problem. Using principles of morality and of intervention, the mediator can make decisions more effectively about the crucial and difficult situations which occur.

As an example of using the principles of morality and of intervention, suppose that one believes that the greatest good for the greatest number is achieved if intervention is permitted in a mediation session only when a person's right to speak interferes with the right of another to be heard. Or again, if you think that intervention is justified on the basis of the conflict principle, then the use of mediation in the landlord/tenant conflict mentioned above would in general terms be justifiable. But no matter what principle one chooses as a basis for action, there is always the question "What sort of intervention should be chosen?" This question leads us into a consideration of the relationship between mediation and the law.

Mediation and the Law

Some assert that the law is the product of what judges and lawyers do. This position is called legal positivism and is very popular among practitioners and legal theorists. Legal positivism can be traced to attitudes derived from scientific and social developments in Western Europe in the seventeenth century. Its most important feature is that the law and morality are separate considerations. The law is not what lawyers and judges *should* do, rather it is what they actually do. For positivists, a law is a law the moment it comes into effect by the processes established in that society. An immoral, illogical or unfair enactment is still a law. They may argue that to refuse to recognize a bad law as a law is like refusing to recognize that an automobile is an automobile simply because it does not work properly. This does not mean that all legal positivists think that bad laws should be enacted or allowed to remain in effect.

Natural law theorists do not agree with this position. For them, the rules and principles by which we must live derive their power from their natural moral force. We cannot make an immoral enactment into a true law any more than we can make a stone float in air. A law is a law because it expresses morality. You cannot make immoral laws, since what is lawful is moral, and vice-versa.

Regardless of how you characterize the law, mediation is clearly a different matter. Where the law seeks to establish standards of behavior against which conduct is measured, sets certain procedures to follow when violations are alleged, and establishes guidelines for retribution, mediation does no more than establish a process whereby disputes can be resolved. The content of the process is theoretically outside of the interest of the mediator. Thus mediation does not seek to establish behavioral norms. The role which a norm of conduct may play is left largely to those in the dispute. Some assert that mediators do have certain rights, e.g., the right to keep order in the meeting, call caucuses, etc. By saying that mediators do not seek to impose behavioral norms, we mean that, in theory at least, the order which the mediator brings to the meeting is of a procedural rather than a contextual nature. Thus, in theory, the mediator's role does not impinge upon the nature of the resolution that the participants agree upon. In this way, mediation can be conceptually distinguished from adjudication, wherein the acts of the judge are clearly meant to affect the resolution that is reached. In practice, the mediator's presence can strongly affect the nature of the outcome, just like the lack of impartiality in a judge can affect the fairness of the judicial process.

Mediation is different from the law in other ways. Mediation seeks only the resolution of a specific conflict. There is no formal system to ensure that future resolutions are consistent with the one just reached. Of course, informal comparisons are often made that are important to a mediation. But in the legal system, decisions are reached which can act as formal guides in the future. These formal guides are called 'precedents' and are an important part of the judicial process. No single mediated agreement is likely to have the effect of precedent-setting ruling.

The law seeks to be fair by removing subjective considerations from positions of influence. Mediation more openly acknowledges the role which relative power plays in any negotiation process. Proponents of mediation often point out that in practice potential litigants negotiate, which brings their relative power into a position of importance which is theoretically absent from the judicial process.

Some argue that the law is nothing more than the instrument of domination by those who can often win the struggle for power. If this is true, then it is not correct to distinguish between the law and mediation by asserting that the former considers only the merits of the case while the latter is the only one of the two which treats relative power as a crucial determinant of the outcome. Those who assert that the law is the instrument of domination are likely to think of mediation and the law as merely different processes by which the same basic result is achieved.

Conclusion

Mediation is a complex event wherein a struggle for dominance of one over the other can be changed to cooperative enterprise. There are many pitfalls into which a mediator can plunge. By carefully delineating the ethical and political issues involved, the mediator can successfully mold a cohesive and consistent approach to the problems of confidentiality, neutrality, and the requirements to report certain acts. The successful use of mediation requires an awareness and clarity of understanding by the mediator of his own ethical framework. Self-awareness and previous thought will prevent unexpected collisions between unexamined values and the necessity for decision.

Review each example and each ethical system. How would you respond and on which bases?

A Case Study:
Moral Dilemma and Ethical Solution
(Based upon an Actual Case)

This case study poses problems of relative power similar to the first example mentioned at the beginning of this chapter. A review of this detailed example will augment your understanding of issues brought forth earlier.

The Situation

John and Mary have been living together for almost one year. They each have two children by previous marriages. On March 1, 1982, they decided to buy a house together, although they had only known each other for about a month. They made an $8000 down payment on the house, of which $5000 belonged to Mary and $3000 to John. About six months after the couple moved into the house, they began to quarrel. At first, they quarreled about money, John complaining that Mary was always spending more than she made, dipping into their mutual funds to make up the differences. Mary insisted that she knew what she was doing, and besides, "What is money for?"

Quarrels about money seemed to lead to an atmosphere of distrust. John began to reduce his contributions to the mutual account and Mary began taking her children out without taking the others along. The children began to quarrel. In the ninth month of the relationship, John struck Mary during a quarrel. During the next two months, quarrels occurred with increasing frequency and John struck Mary during many of these. Mary sometimes threw things at John, occasionally instigating a violent interchange. Finally, Mary moved out and sought a mediator.

When Mary spoke to the mediator, she had found a furnished apartment for herself and her two children. She seemed intent upon ending the relationship with John. She said that her main concerns were for her safety, (the children had not been threatened, she said), her furniture, her share of the house, his share of mutually acquired bills, and the major appliances which she said she had acquired prior to beginning the relationship with John (this case took place in a community property state). She had a very pressing need for the furniture.

Mary's stance on the house and bills was, by her own account, softened considerably because John had possession of the furniture. This gave John extra power. Instead of demanding her full share of the proceeds from the sale (or other disposition) of the house, Mary was willing to take 50% of the total net worth of the house. She claimed that the furniture was worth $15,000, and had been entirely purchased before she and John had established the relationship.

The mediator faced a dilemma. Should the furniture be allowed to remain in John's possession and Mary be allowed to be in an inferior bargaining position? Or should the mediator attempt to equalize the relative power of the parties? By allowing John to retain the furniture, the mediator (or society or the law) is allowing John a bargaining advantage by virtue of the fact that Mary has moved from the premises, perhaps because John has successfully intimidated her. On the other hand, the mediator may violate his commitment to neutrality by intervening on Mary's behalf.

The mediator's commitment to neutrality is a promise to the client that means, in part, that he will not advocate a particular point of view held by one of the parties. This commitment is in conflict with the commitment to preventing either party from taking unfair advantage during the mediation, a commitment that is held by some mediators. The moral problem is the dilemma that derives from two moral principles which demand contradictory action. If the mediator is to remain neutral, he can take no action to equalize the power between the parties. If the mediator fails to act on Mary's behalf, he may be rewarding an abuser's tactics.

Commonly, mediators (and others) would, in this situation, refer Mary to an attorney who would act as her advocate. This may be an appropriate response, although other appropriate responses also exist (i.e., entering into the mediation with obtaining the furniture as one of Mary's goals). Yet the discovery of a strategy is not the purpose, but a by-product of the ethical inquiry. The ethical inquiry asks us to justify the choice we do make. If the choice is to initiate mediation, why was it made? Should we rationalize on the basis of the act or the rule, deontologically or consequentially?

Let us attempt to justify our choice based upon consequentialist agreements. The choice is to begin mediation without first trying to equalize the power between the parties. Only in the particular circumstances now under consideration, and only because of the by-and-large favorable consequences which would result, we should begin the mediation. We will consider the circumstances and the consequences. We will assume that the only choices of action available to the mediator were 1) proceeding with mediation without Mary having benefit of legal counsel or 2) referring Mary to legal counsel and refusing to proceed until that act is accomplished by Mary.

Considering the Circumstances

Assume that active legal intervention would initially cost Mary $500.00. Let us also assume that Mary claimed that she could not raise $500, or even $250 in less than eight weeks, and even then only with difficulty and by leaving some bills unpaid. Failure to pay her creditors would make her more of a risk to potential creditors, making future purchases more difficult. She claimed that free legal services were unavailable to her. Furthermore, active legal intervention might produce hostilities on John's part. His possession of the furniture and other of Mary's possessions would allow him to damage, hide or sell them in retaliation. For Mary to prove that John undertook actions of this sort would be difficult. Mary could not conceive of any way to observe what John might do with the furniture.

In addition, we will assume that a three-month wait would be required before a pre-trial hearing could take place. Mary's legal counselor advised her that the furniture could be removed from the house by either party without a pre-trial hearing. John's attorney had indicated to Mary that John said the furniture was his. Mary had tried to remove the furniture. John's daughter was home and called John at work. John returned home and an ugly confrontation ensued. Mary did not get the furniture. Mary's emotional resources for dealing with the tension were becoming depleted. Her ability to fight could not last at peak levels through a trial. She quaked at just the thought of a hearing.

Considering the Consequences

The high cost of retaining legal counsel relative to Mary's economic status placed strong barriers across that path. The consequences of taking that path, then, were such as to make it undesirable. The economic costs outweighed the benefits. Had Mary's relative economic status allowed for an investment of $500 (or more, as may be required in circumstances of this type), then hiring legal counsel could have positive consequences, from Mary's viewpoint. Had she been able to obtain free legal counsel, the lowered cost would also contribute to the desirability.

The increased possibility of John damaging, hiding or selling the furniture in retaliation for Mary's attempts to gain control of it is a factor that must be taken into account. Acts of compellence and deterrence, often engaged in by attorneys jockeying for position, produce mixed results. Compliance and non-compliance, even outright defiance, all occur. Court orders that prohibit a party from engaging this type of activity rely upon a willingness to comply, not the actual ability to enforce such an instruction. If John were angered by the order, he might well do the opposite.

Time is also an important factor. Hearings before a judge or jury are typically accompanied by intentional delay, crowded dockets, illnesses, etc. Time pressures us emotionally by forcing us to sustain undesirable emotional states. Increased time commitments often bring increased economic costs and competition between the conflict and other opportunities for a limited supply of one's money and time. In Mary's case, living without the furniture she had painstakingly collected made her life unpleasant. She felt displaced, and could not get rid of her memory of dashed hopes. These feelings intensified with the passage of time.

Why Consider the Consequences?

The deontological theorist cannot consider consequences as the basis for moral decision-making. As an extreme example, he cannot consider any consequences arising from killing that might justify or condemn such behavior. No consequence, and no positive balance of good over evil justifies killing or not killing. If killing is wrong, it is wrong in itself. But how do we arrive at this conclusion? What connection is there between our experience and our ethical principles? This connection must be through consequences. If murder is (always) bad, or sometimes bad, we know this because of, say, the instability which arises in the social order from (some) killing. Conversely, if some killing is justified, we know this because of the consequences that follow from the act. Cutting us off from any consequences isolates us from one source of knowledge. This does not seem desirable, in part because good consequences of action contribute to desirable state of being. If we do not orient ourselves to the evaluation of consequences, we do not maximize our opportunities to achieve desirable consequences, insofar as that method of evaluation might guide our behavior.

Why Consider Only the Act?

Some theorists argue that there are rules, derived consequentially or through some deontological method, that hold true across a broad range of circumstances. At most, only a few circumstances are so unusual as to demand an individualized evaluation. Individualized evaluation of each set of circumstances is not only unnecessary but time-consuming and perhaps hopelessly intricate, since there are no rules which we can apply. A new "rule" must be found for each situation. Some act theorists argue that only "rules of thumb," that is, general guidelines, exist by which we can evaluate given circumstances. This type of act theorist is really a "general-rule theorist."

Rule theorists also object that having no rules produces social chaos. They contend that trying to live as an act utilitarian would lead to misjudgments of consequences so often that the theory would not yield the desirable consequences it seems to assure.[4] Consequences are often hard to predict. Without rules to act as guidelines, not only would we have to invest a significant amount of time in decision-making, but variations in decisions from one person to another (and from time to time by the same person) make social orderliness difficult to achieve.

These are both powerful objections. Let us say in response that the adoption of rules does not prohibit individuals from making utilitarian considerations regarding killing, promise-keeping, lying and the like. Act utilitarianism acknowledges the freedom that people already in fact exercise. Promoting the idea that a person should not kill or break a promise because those acts violate rules, does not promote a thoughtful, rational individual, but a type of automaton. The idea that each act ought to be considered on its own terms promotes individual responsibility for moral and ethical decision-making. Short cuts are not necessarily good ideas.

Secondly, act utilitarianism, because it does promote individuality, will produce variations in results. This is productive of social disorder only to those who seek a high degree of conformity in outcomes. The disadvantage produced by variations is an advantage to those who seek to promote an individualized social norm, as distinct from a collective one.

In Conclusion

Naturally, this debate could be extended, the various points of view more fully developed and new points of view introduced. Hopefully, it is clear that mediators have not only moral obligations, but ethical ones as well. The values we express are usually communicated better when the clarity of reason is present.

You may ask yourself questions like, "Do I wish to promote individualized standards of conduct or communal standards?" "What rules of behavior apply to the mediator in what sorts of circumstances?" Debating these issues with your fellow mediators can produce heightened awareness of the difficult moral and ethical dilemmas which we all face as mediators.

Notes

1. Frankena, William K., "Ethics", Prentice Hall, 1973.
2. Arendt, Hannah, "Origins of Totalitarianism," Harcourt, Brace & World, 1966.
3. Feinburg, Joel, "Social Philosophy," Prentice Hall, 1973, p. 33.
4. Sartorius, Rolf E., "Individual Conduct and Social Norms," Dickensen Publishing Co., 1975, p. 14.

X. Crisis Intervention and the Mediator

A crisis occurs when unusual stress in an individual's life temporarily renders him unable to direct his life effectively. "Crisis Intervention" or "Crisis Management" is the skillful intrusion into a personal crisis to defuse a potentially disastrous situation before physical and/or emotional destruction results.

The potential for client stress and tension may be at maximum levels before, during, or immediately following a mediation session. At these times, the client often experiences extreme feelings of fear, anger, grief, hostility, helplessness, hopelessness, and/or alienation from his self-concept, his family and society. He may experience a pervasive sense of anxiety which produces disorganized, chaotic thinking. The person may feel overwhelmed and unable to move in any direction. The client will look to the mediator to provide structure in a world which seems to be falling apart. The mediator becomes privy to the most private concerns and feelings of the client. He is often required by circumstances to take emotional control until the client is able to restore his own coping mechanisms and regain self-control.

Often, the role of mediator must be broadened to include Crisis Intervention. The mediator's success as a Crisis Intervener will determine if the mediation process can continue. The mediator's sensitivity and attention to the client's immediate needs predict his ability to manage the temporary disorientation. Until the crisis is past, the mediation cannot continue.

This broadened role is sometimes foreign and uncomfortable for the mediator. Being cast in an unfamiliar setting can easily produce heightened anxiety and stress for the unskilled intervener. He may feel inadequately trained or ill-prepared to deal with emotional crises. Out of his own sense of helplessness he might decide to abort the session or to ignore the crisis and continue trying to follow normal mediation procedure in the hope that maybe things will "straighten out soon." Both actions are dangerous and counter-productive.

A mediator does not have to become a psychotherapist to understand or to use the techniques of effective Crisis Intervention. The emphasis of Crisis Intervention is on immediate response, rather than on long or short term counseling. The goal of the mediator in this context is to offer "emotional first aid" to the client before these upsets escalate into violence and trauma. If a crisis occurs, the mediator has two major tasks: a) to reduce emotional trauma, and b) to return the client to the pre-crisis level of functioning.

To accomplish both tasks the intervener must understand the immediate motivation of the sufferer, which is rooted in his current perception of the world. Without this appreciation of the client's perception of reality, the mediator cannot effectively deal with the behavior.

It is useful to review certain principles of human behavior and human motivation as background for exploring maladaptive crisis-behavior. In their books, Sherif and Sherif developed a

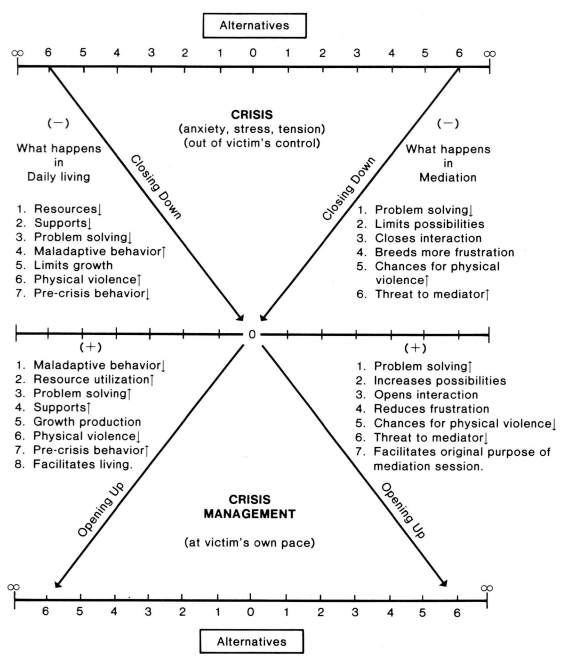

Figure 46. Crisis Management and Mediation (James L. Greenstone).

series of ten principles in an effort to explain the origin of human social motivation. A brief enumeration of their principles and some explanations and comments are appropriate.

1. *Experience and behavior constitute a unity.*
2. *Behavior follows central psychological structuring.*

    Behavior is, in fact, the consequence of central structuring or patterning of external and internal impulses; hence, it is the unity of experience and action. Action is not a direct function of external stimuli or internal impulses. Behavior follows the central organization of all of these factors.

3. *Psychological structuring is jointly determined by external and internal factors.*

    External factors are stimulating situations outside of the individual. They include objects, events, cultural norms, other people and groups.

    Internal factors include motives, attitudes, emotions and personal history. The functionally interrelated external and internal factors operating at a given time constitute the frame of reference for the ensuing reaction. Observed behavior can be more easily understood and evaluated when studied within its appropriate frame of reference or system of relations.

4. *Internal factors are inferred from behavior.* The intervener's data consists of items of observed behavior, both verbal and nonverbal, and identifiable external stimuli. Motives, attitudes and experience are inferred from observed behavior in specific situations. Overt actions, words spoken or written, subtle body and facial expressions are all behavior. The unity of experience and behavior is again implied.

5. *The psychological tendency is to the structuring of experience in understandable patterns.*

6. *External stimuli set limits of feasible alternatives in internal psychological structuring.*

7. *Unstructured stimuli increase alternatives in psychological structuring.*

8. *The more unstructured or uncertain the situation, the greater the relative contribution of both internal and external factors in the frame of reference.* To the frightened person in the dark, there are many more hostile movements in the shrubbery. The more uncertain and unstructured the stimuli, the greater the effects of social influences (personal suggestion, group demand) in psychological structuring. This has been demonstrated in experiments by Ash in the influence of peer pressure on perception.

    As an individual becomes aware through his senses of the external and internal events affecting him, he must interpret them in a manner that permits him to react consistently with his belief structure. Much behavior is motivated by a perceived need to understand and control the interpersonal environment. One major way to control the environment is to interpret the world in line with one's internal psychological structure. As long as stability between belief and reality exist, the individual ego is satisfied. When this equilibrium is destroyed, through unsupported attitudes, new norms, or disagreements with those important to us, the individual will seek to reestablish the structure. The theory of cognitive dissonance (Festinger) postulates a need for consonance between belief and action. He may do so by seeking new knowledge, accepting new norms, or by blaming others for "forsaking proven ways." Whatever the method chosen, the self-image must be protected. If too great a disparity is perceived between what is held to be true and what is demonstrated to be true, the individual may devolve into crisis.

Self-image is the way an individual sees himself and believes that others see him. This image guides his thinking and behavior. Observed behavior then is a manifestation of the self-image which is constantly seeking a balanced state between the external influences and the internal attitudes which are part of the psychological structure.

9. *Various elements in the frame of reference have differing relative weights.* Even though all the elements that function as parts within a frame of reference influence other parts, a certain element or cluster of elements are preeminent in determining the main character of the structure. These limiting, weighty factors are referred to as the "main anchorages" in the frame of reference.

10. *Psychological activity is selective.* We perceive only a small portion of objects or people in a given time and space. Individuals quickly tend to single out objects and persons in their environment that they love or hate, depend on or fear, esteem or despise. The selection of these objects or persons is premised upon personal motives, attitudes and preoccupations which are superordinate at the time. For example, the thought of food or drink is relatively unimportant until hunger or thirst is felt. Identification of the operative motivational factors becomes the key for the intervener. If he can come to understand what desires, attitudes, preoccupations and interests are operating for the victim at the time of crisis, he can become more effective in his dealing with the victim's crisis. The frightened person is quick to see threatening signs in his surroundings. A person who feels "let down" by friends becomes sensitive even to slight insinuations which may pass unnoticed during a period of greater confidence and stability.

At times, a person finds himself not only lacking external structure, but also lacking the customary anchorages for experience. When he is unable to establish landmarks in his life, he searches, sometimes frantically, to find secure anchorage. When social ties with friends, loved ones, or associates are disrupted, he gropes in uncertainty. His feeling of self-identity is shaken. Such factors are significant in understanding the development of self. It has been repeatedly shown that personality integration and the development of goal-oriented behavior are strongly conditioned upon the existence of stable referents.

How are these ten principles of human social motivation related to a discussion of Crisis Intervention? First, all behavior can be viewed on a continuum extending from what is called normal behavior to that which is considered to be abnormal. Normal behavior is seen as a way of acting that is representative of the relevant social norm. However, this norm changes from time to time. Indeed, there is no absolute norm or standard that remains the same all of the time for everyone. When we classify a certain behavior as abnormal, it is because those actions do not allow the individual to adapt to the needs he is experiencing in his everyday living (Rosenbluh, 1974). Such patterns of behavior are usually both socially unacceptable and ineffectual.

Second, as was stated earlier, behavior is determined by several interrelated elements. Each element affects what a person chooses to do or not do. One such factor is individual perception of the external world. Expectations, needs, social stimuli and personal history affect such perceptions. Each of us has developed assumptions which color and determine our behavior. We function in accordance with these deeply-held beliefs. This may explain why crisis-producing events for one person might be quite tolerable for another.

Frequently the conflict between social norms and individual needs precipitates a crisis. The rules that a society makes inviolable have a profound influence upon our feelings. Sometimes these rules are stress-producing even to the point of crisis. The definitions will vary in relation to the surrounding social, economic and political conditions and may impinge more strongly at certain times than others. The individual when caught between his own behavior (which he perceives as normal) and societal definitions (which label his actions as abnormal) is in danger of personal crisis. Nowhere is this seen more frequently than in domestic relations conflicts, especially when one partner sees religious or social norms as being violated by the other partner.

Recognition of Maladaptive Behavior

A mediator's effectiveness is strengthened through the identification of those individuals who are about to experience crisis. The person who is prone to crisis can be characterized by several indicators. These include:

1. An alienation from lasting and meaningful personal relationships.
2. An inability to utilize life support systems such as family, friends and social groups.
3. A difficulty in learning from life experience so that the individual continues to make the same mistakes.
4. A history of previously experienced crises which have not been effectively resolved.
5. Feelings of low self-esteem and/or a history of emotional disorders.
6. Provocative, impulsive behavior resulting from unresolved inner conflicts.
7. Poor marital relationships.
8. Excessive use of drugs, including alcohol abuse.
9. Marginal income.
10. Lack of regular, fulfilling work.
11. Unusual or frequent physical injuries.
12. Frequent changes in address.

Events Which May Precipitate a Crisis

There are a number of events which may precipitate a crisis in the life of an individual. These include:

1. An accident in the home.
2. An automobile accident with or without physical injury.
3. Being arrested, appearing in court (anticipating a mediation session).
4. Changes in job situation and income.
5. Changes in school status involving either promotion or demotion.
6. Death of a significant person in one's life.
7. Divorce or separation.
8. A delinquency episode.
9. Physical illness or acute episodes of mental disorder.
10. Actual loss or impending loss of something significant in one's life.

Individuals who seem most crisis-prone are those who are sensitive to relatively minor stress. Of course, the likelihood of crisis is increased when many stresses occur simultaneously or in rapid succession. The so-called "Life Change Index" is an excellent indicator of crisis potential. While a particular, stressful situation may not induce crisis, a combination of several such stressful events may push the individual to the crisis point.

It is now obvious that our effectiveness as mediators requires an ability to recognize when a crisis is occurring. People indicate crises in different ways. Some cry out and become very obvious about their suffering. Others may withdraw and become depressed. A person in crisis may evidence any of the following mental states as characterized by their verbal responses:

1. Bewilderment: "I've never felt this way before."
2. Danger: "I'm so nervous and frightened."
3. Impasse: "I feel stuck. Nothing I do seems to help."
4. Confusion: "I can't think clearly."
5. Desperation: "I've just got to do something!"
6. Apathy: "Nothing I do seems to help, so why bother anymore?"
7. Helplessness: "I can't take care of myself!"
8. Urgency: "I need help now!"
9. Discomfort: "I feel miserable. I'm restless and unsettled."

The following vignettes serve to illustrate how differently people display maladaptive behavior.

1) Mr. Smith: I want visitation with the children more than one weekend a month. Can't she understand how important my children are to me?

Mediator: Seeing your children means a great deal to you?

Mr. Smith: How can she do that to me! I've raised those kids. I've carpooled every day, paid for their schooling, babysat with them, cuddled them when they cried or were sick. I'm the one they come to when there's a problem. My little boy needs to have me around.

Mediator: It sounds like you need him too.

Mr. Smith: All of a sudden everything is in such a muddle. I may not have been the best husband, but I'm a damn good father. My world is falling apart. My wife is leaving; I'll only see my children one night once a month. I can't concentrate on my job. I . . . I . . . feel terribly alone! I . . . feel . . . I can't handle this. I feel so cut off and helpless. . . .

2) During the mediation session Mrs. Jones becomes withdrawn, shy, passive and uncommunicative. She is communicating. She has sunk into her own internal world, a safer one, she thinks, than the real world. Her message is in her passivity and silence.

3) The mediation session has ended. An agreement was reached and signed by the two parties involved in the dispute. The initiator has left and the respondent remains seated. She holds back the tears for a few moments and then begins crying. The tears are suddenly replaced with screams. Her rage intensifies and she begins pounding her fists on her lap.

In each of the above cases, the parties to the mediation experienced stress that they were no longer able to manage using their normal methods of coping. Each suffered a heightened degree of helplessness, hopelessness, frustration, fear or alienation—all of which are expected reactions of those who experience crisis.

A well-trained intervener, regardless of his academic background or professional status, must and can effectively defuse the trauma and assist any of the above victims in returning to their precrisis level of functioning.

In reviewing what has been covered, it may be helpful to refer to the Crisis Cube (Greenstone, 1977). The cube is a pictorial, three-dimensional representation of how a crisis develops and the effects of both proper and improper intervention. (Fig. 47)

Crisis, in general, will usually follow the patterns outlined. Stress and minor crises are inherent in daily living and people develop problem solving techniques to function effectively. However, when stress and tension begin to build in our lives because of the occurrence of unusual, sudden and unexpected events, we may find that our usually effective coping mechanisms do not provide the expected relief.

Stress continues to mount and the crisis intensifies. The victim will then resort to various trial and error problem-solving efforts in an attempt to develop new ways of subduing the problem. This usually does not work either, and panic sets in. The behavior of the victim becomes increasingly maladaptive. Maladaptive behavior is distinguished from mentally-ill behavior by the fact that without the crisis, the maladaptive behavior would not exist. A maladaptive response is directly connected to the crisis.

Intervention Procedure

Effective Crisis Intervention consists of five components: immediacy, control, assessment, disposition, and referral and follow-up.

Immediacy—A crisis is self-limiting. It will cease even if intervention does not occur. However, we must consider the potential personal and/or emotional destruction that could result if the crisis were allowed to run its course. Effective intervention must begin immediately. The time to intervene is "now." The mediator must attempt to relieve anxiety, prevent further disorientation and insure that the victim does not harm himself or others. This must be done quickly and effectively. It might best be done in caucus.

Control—The second major component of Crisis Intervention is control-taking. Because the crisis victim is often not in control of his life during the crisis experience, the mediator must assume control of the total situation. On the one hand, there is chaos, disorganization and confusion, a state in which all possibilities become vague. On the other hand, there is an over-focus in which the victim's preoccupation with his problems narrows the scope to such an extent that he is unable to see any alternatives. The mere presence of an authoritative figure who is seen as strong, stable and supportive can help the victim consider other options.

Sometimes control may be accomplished passively simply by the presence of the intervener. Other circumstances may necessitate that the mediator take control in a more insistent manner. Physical force is not used except as a last resort, and only then in a judicious, well-planned way by those properly trained to use it. The concept of control does not mean brute or physical force, simply firmness and direction. For example, it is possible to guide a person through carefully planned hand, eye and/or foot movements without ever physically touching the victim. Similarly, it is possible to quiet an upset individual through proper voice control and without the need for physical persuasion. The purpose of assuming control is not to conquer or overwhelm the victim, but rather to help reorder the chaos that exists in his world at the moment of crisis.

By taking the controlling position, the mediator provides the needed structure until the victim is able to provide it for himself. People in crisis will respond to structure and to those who represent it if they sense that the attempt is sincere rather than merely a technique.

111

CRISIS CUBE

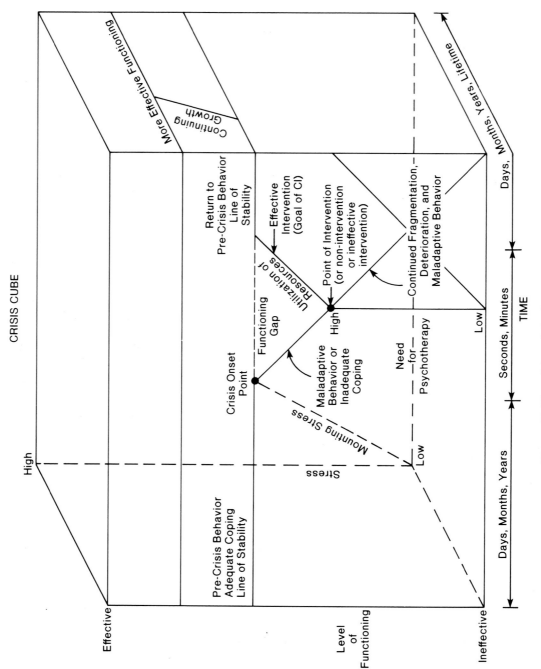

Figure 47. (Copyright © J. L. Greenstone, 1977.)

112

Specific ways to gain control of a crisis situation will vary depending on the skills and abilities of the interveners. The task allows wide latitude for creativity. Some possible ways of taking control include:

1. Creating a loud noise to gain attention.
2. Speaking in a quieter tone than the victim.
3. Breaking eye contact between two disputants. When eye contact is broken, tension is temporarily reduced.
4. Making an odd request to divert attention.
5. Directing and arranging the pattern of standing or sitting to gain the attention of the victim.
6. Using the mediator's own personal presence; his own strength, control, structure and calm in the crisis situation may exert the control needed.
7. Using clarity in introductory statements. The directions, opening questions and other information that are given to the victim will often assist in gaining and maintaining control.

Regardless of the methods chosen to gain control, the attitude of the mediator must be one of being in control at all times; otherwise, any method selected will be of little value.

Assessment—Assessment is the third component of an effective intervention. An on-the-spot evaluation must be done. It must be quick, accurate and comprehensive enough to give a total assessment of the victim. A lengthy life history is inappropriate in crisis intervention. The focus is on the present crisis and the events that precipitated it. The mediator must concern himself with the following questions:

1. What is troubling the victim now?
2. Why did he go into crisis at this particular time?
3. Which problem among the several that may be present is of immediate concern to the mediator?
4. Which problem must be dealt with first before other problems can be handled?
5. Which problem among the ones presented can be most immediately solved?
6. What variables will hinder the problem-solving process?
7. How can the mediator implement the most effective help in the shortest amount of time?

Short, direct questions are often the most helpful in the assessment process. Such questions might include, "How are you feeling?"; "What is troubling you?"; "What is making you fearful?". Questions should be asked singly with sufficient time allowed for the victim to answer without feeling pushed. Bombarding him with many questions will increase his confusion. Some people feel uncomfortable with silence. An intervener must learn to accept his discomfort with silence and recognize its usefulness in the intervention process.

The intervener might make statements describing how the behavior of the victim is perceived. "I can see you are very angry," might not only bring agreement but also an outpouring of feelings within which the crisis event is revealed. A victim will usually tell the intervener if his assessment is inaccurate. "No, it's not anger that I'm feeling; it's total frustration with my whole world. I can't hold anything together anymore. . . . I want to reach a settlement today, but I can't seem to concentrate."

The mediator's statement must demonstrate caring and the intent to be helpful. A periodic interruption of the victim's verbalizations by the mediator for clarification will serve several functions, including reminding the sufferer of the mediator's interest and concern for his problem and permitting the mediator to check the accuracy and understanding of what the victim has said or meant by a statement.

In the assessment process, the mediator must try to identify the nature of the events precipitating the crisis. Is it loss or impending loss, a change of life style? The mediator must assess both the actual and the symbolic meanings of whatever has happened to the victim, remembering that perception triggers crisis more often than facts.

The mediator must attend to what the victim says and what he does. He must also be aware of what the victim has not done and what would normally be expected under such circumstances. Often body language and nonverbal behavior become a more important source of information than the verbalizations of the individual.

The mediator's personal attributes contribute to his effectiveness. He must be reassuring and calm. He must be empathic and attentive. He must be supportive and willing to reach out to the victim, both emotionally and physically as needed. He must be concerned and maintain a caring attitude that conveys his willingness to listen. A person in crisis normally will open up to an intervener if he feels that the intervener is approachable.

Disposition—The next step in the intervention procedure is to help the crisis victim effectively manage the particular problem that he is experiencing and to develop, or reinstate, adaptive behavior which will allow more realistic and effective functioning. The victim may need help in finding better methods of coping or more effective ways of expressing the stress and inner tension that he feels. Crisis Intervention actively assists the victim to identify and mobilize his own resources as well as those of family and friends. Even though solutions may not be available on the spot, the mediator must hold out the realistic hope that such solutions are possible. When the stress is abated, the mediator can help both parties open options that might reduce the stress to an even greater degree. Heightened stress serves to close down options, producing tunnel vision. When effective intervention occurs and the parties are able to resume the mediation, there is an increased receptivity to exploring options, to creativity in thinking and problem solving. The parties have experienced success by temporarily overcoming a challenging and disturbing emotional state.

Referral and follow-up—Referral and follow-up are the final steps in Crisis Intervention. While the mediator has as his main concern the immediate crisis problems rather than those that may be chronic and not immediately pressing, he may still direct the person in crisis toward ongoing assistance for these chronic situations.

General Guidelines for Effective Intervention into Crisis Situations

1. Attempt to limit the personal disorganization that the victim is expressing by calming him and relieving as much of the anxiety and stress as possible.
2. If possible, remove the victim from the crisis situation and provide a place for him to relax and compose himself.
3. Remain confident and be firm and reasonable at all times.
4. Do not agree or disagree with the victim. The way he perceives the world at this time in his life is real for him.

5. Encourage family members to be with the victim if appropriate. Some family members may be disruptive or in crisis themselves. The mediator must assess the potential helpfulness of all significant others before bringing them into contact with the victim.
6. Encourage the victim to relax and to tell what is troubling him.
7. Help the victim to see his crisis as temporary rather than chronic. Recovery is usually quicker when the problems are viewed in this way rather than as an unsolvable situation which may never be fully resolved.
8. Allow the victim to speak freely and to ventilate his feelings.
9. In a multiple victim situation (such as a family dispute) allow each person to speak without interruption by the other parties. Establish the ground rules immediately and insist that they be followed.
10. Avoid unnecessary interruptions while the crisis victim is speaking.
11. Build a sense of structure to which the victim can relate as you talk with him. In crisis, he may see his life as chaotic and out of his control. The more he understands the nature of his crisis experience and the more quickly he can secure a sense of structure for himself, the more quickly he will recover and be able to function effectively.
12. Avoid arguing with the victim. There are many ways of viewing a situation. The role of the mediator is to help direct the problem solving, not to judge or badger.

The reader is urged to use and to study the recommended procedure rather than be limited by it. Creativity, judgment, response to one's intuition in a given situation, and adaptation of procedures to one's own profession are all tools of responsible, skillful Crisis Intervention.

XI. Safety and Weapons

Neither the mediator's certificate of training nor his professional diploma or good intentions will stop bullets, avoid physical or verbal attacks, or guarantee the absence of knives in a mediation session. What the mediator does before, during and after a session is the key to preventing the occurrence of tragedies related, but not limited to the possibilities mentioned above. Recognition by the mediator that safety concerns must be more than just philosophized about in professional circles, is an important start in the right direction. The reality of weapons exists. The reality of compromised mediator safety also exists. The seriousness given this area by those who work in this field and who study this manual may not only save mediation sessions from deterioration and default, but also save the life of the mediator and/or the parties to the dispute. While most of the mediation done in centers today will not involve threats or actual violence, one such incident would be enough to convince most of us of the need for information about how to handle such situations. The experienced mediator, sooner or later, will run into situations in which the potential for violence is present. If that mediator's experience has taught him/her the value of considering the safety factors in each mediation session, the chances of avoiding the serious consequences of such encounters is increased markedly.

This is not an area of which to be afraid. It is an area that deserves your recognition and attention. Many trainees report some trepidation when, in training, they are confronted with the subject of safety and weapons as part of their curriculum. Often the novice enters the realm of dispute mediation much as he or she would enter a social club or a community activity. The expectations are that those with whom he will work will be as calm, collected and civilized as he, and that the client will exercise the needed control of self during a session. This may or not be the case, depending on the heightened state of emotions present.

Much of what the mediator does in preparing for the session, much of what is done by the mediator during the session, and even what is done after the session has ended, will make a difference in the area of safety. A successful session or sessions may well be the result of careful safety planning as well as careful planning of mediation strategies. If the concern for safety factors in a mediation session becomes as much a second nature to the mediator as any other negotiation skill, the likelihood of positive outcomes is increased.

Begin by planning for trouble. If you have planned for what could happen and it does not occur, the mediator is ahead of the game. If no planning has been done and problems arise, the results could be devastating to all concerned. As the next few paragraphs are read and studied, begin to orient yourself to a mode of safety consciousness. This consciousness should include concerns for the safety of the parties to the dispute, the mediator or mediators, those who may be recipients of the consequences of what the parties to the dispute do, and even the office staff in the agency to which you are attached. What you do or not do may affect them all. The object of safety planning is to prevent and to facilitate all at the same time. By "prevent" is meant the prevention of the potential for violence that often accompanies disputes between persons who are functioning at a high emotional pitch. By "facilitate" is meant the facilitation of the mediation session, which is the central focus of all present. Much of what the mediator will do in the realm of safety will be done almost automatically after the skills are learned and adapted. While probably not always occupying the central attention of the mediator, the procedures should be followed as consistently as one would follow basic procedures for beginning a session, caucusing, negotiating or writing up a contract. Every session brings with it its own set of unique factors. Nothing is ever the same. Application of all factors, therefore, must adjust to compensate for differences. Regardless of the differences, the mediator must be quick to spot, to sense, to see, the potential for problems which are over and above those which would usually lend themselves to the mediation process.

Probably the mediator's best tool to detect potential violence or the presence of weapons is his/her own internal communication and sensing capabilities. All too often, we know more in fact than we are willing to allow ourselves to acknowledge. All of us at one time or another have experienced inklings; partial awarenesses which are not clear or complete in terms of our central awareness. It may be a sense that all is not well or that there is more present in the room than meets the eye. The successful mediator is one who has developed the use of these sensing devices in the skillful art of negotiating. The mediator who develops these same sensors in the area of personal and client safety will probably be around long enough to be successful in the art of negotiating. Do not overlook any message that comes to your senses. They each mean something. Sometimes you will find that the meanings are nonessential in that particular setting. Often the reverse is true. Sensing that a husband and wife do not get along may not indicate that any special action on the part of the mediator is needed other than the mediation itself. Conversely, sensing that the actions, stances, verbalizations, and the like may indicate the possibility that one or both of the parties intend to do injury to the other, is a real cause for concern on the part of the mediator and an indicator that quick, definitive and effective action must be taken. What the mediator in this situation will do largely depends on his/her particular style and capabilities in handling such matters. But regardless of style, each mediator will know that the potential for violence exists and that the mediation process cannot begin, continue or culminate until the matters of safety and personal well-being are dealt with. To overlook clues about clients is potentially disastrous regardless of whether or not these clues are signals about the issues at dispute or about safety in the session. Develop your sensing capabilities. Fine tune them to give accurate information. Be open to the information that the senses provide, and be ready to respond as needed to the information gained. This is not an appeal to paranoia, any more than recognizing the symptoms of physical illness is an appeal to hypochondria. The appeal is to the fullness of training and of experience that can be the difference between success and failure in our profession.

Effective response in violent or potentially violent situations is dependent on knowledge. It is also highly dependent on the degree to which the mediator does what is necessary and then *only* what is necessary. "Over-kill," to use a popular expression, is as costly as failing to respond at all. There is no need to panic. There is only the need to respond, and to respond correctly. Do only what is needed; nothing more. Correct the situation as you see it and move on as effectively as possible. Remember that part of the role of the mediator is to take and to maintain control. As the person in charge, the clients will respond to you if they know, by your actions and words, that you clearly know what you are doing and have the confidence to do it. Trying to bluff your way through a situation or attempting to be nondirective when obvious direction is needed, may prove to be folly for all.

Why do people resort to weapons? The specific reasons are as assorted as the people themselves. The more general motivations, however, may result from extreme frustration, fear, personal feelings of inadequacy and the like. As perceived stress increases, each of us looks for ways to release and to reduce the pressure and pain experienced. Some ways are more adaptive than others. Some ways are clearly intolerable and unacceptable in our society. Jogging around the block, taking a hot bath, mediating a dispute or merely choosing to respond differently in order to reduce the unwanted stress are usually seen as somewhat adaptive and positive. Filing a law suit, having a few drinks or maybe a few more, speaking badly about the person with whom you are in conflict, harboring grudges, fighting in a courtroom are all socially acceptable in our society as ways open to us in dealing with such problems.

Violence is another matter. It is generally not accepted, at least not for its own sake. Suffice it to say that, when either because of reduced intelligence, options, alternatives, motivation, skills and resources, and because of increased stress leading to feelings of frustration, emotional castration or loss, the potential for resorting to the use of weapons increases among those with these experiences. Others may resort to violent attacks and the use of weapons because of sociopathic inclinations. These tendencies are seen in those whose life structure is amoral rather than immoral and asocial rather than antisocial. Most people do not function in this sociopathic, non-conscienced way, and the mediator will most likely meet the former rather than the latter. The use of weapons is a response to a situation in which or for which the responding party sees no other alternative. Such a response may be more symptomatic than problematic. Regardless, it cannot be allowed to jeopardize the intent of mediation or the other parties, and must be prevented or at least stopped. It is certainly within the realm of the mediator's role to help the violent party to develop other ways of expressing and handling the stress and frustration that is experienced.

Office Arrangement

A good place to start to consider safety factors involved in mediation is the arrangement of the mediator's office or other area actually used for mediation. Certain basic preventive actions seem to offer the best results. Arrangement of tables, chairs and desks in the room should be such as to allow easy exit from the room by either of the disputing parties without having to go over, around or through the mediator. Generally, the backs of the clients should be toward the main door to the mediation room. The mediator, then, faces the doorway with the clients before him.

Many mediators use a table across which to do the mediating. Round, square or rectangular shapes may be used. The selection of the shape of the table may vary according to the specific situation, mediator style, or agency purchase. The mediator must choose the shape for a reason. A round table, for example, could be very good for disputes between several parties. If where a person sits is an issue, the round table could be the solution. If multiple parties, such as parents and children, are involved, where you desire them to speak directly to each other, the rectangular table, conference type, can be useful. The square table can be valuable with two parties and/or with two mediators. It can provide a small, intimate setting that can enhance the parties' attempts at consensus.

At times, no table at all may be used. Such cases include times when distance between mediator and clients is a factor. Without the desk or table between them, a greater closeness may be achieved. The table or desk provides a barrier. Barriers can be good or bad, depending on what you are trying to accomplish. From the standpoint of safety considerations, the barrier of the table or desk can prove valuable in potentially hostile situations. Use these items to your advantage.

If there is a reason to suspect problems of a violent nature, or if you want to check the situation before you decide what to do, sit behind the desk as a protection if it is needed. Let parties to a dispute sit across a table from each other, rather than on the same side, if you have a hunch that violence may erupt between them. The distance allows the mediator time to react effectively should violence occur.

Additionally, avoid having anything but essential objects on the mediation table. Papers, pencils or pens and relevant paperwork should suffice for most mediations. Anything that potentially can be used as a weapon should be eliminated from the immediate surroundings of the mediation session. This can be done easily prior to bringing in and seating the clients. The office interior can be checked by the mediator and proper precautions taken.

Seating Parties

Seating the parties to a dispute must also be considered from a safety standpoint. Parties should be brought in and seated so that the person who is most likely to become violent does not have to pass the other party on his way in. To accomplish this, seat the one least likely to become violent in the chair furthest from the doorway. Then bring in the other party and put this person closer to the door. A secondary advantage in this is that should the second party be unable or unwilling to remain in the session, he can leave without posing any problems for the mediator or for the other party.

Generally speaking, the mediator should follow the parties into the mediation room rather than leading the way or ushering them in as you might if they were visiting you in your home as guests. Not only does this avoid having the mediator's back to a client at any time, but also the mediator can view the clients from the rear, thereby discovering additional information that might be useful from a safety standpoint or in mediation. For instance, apparent hard bulges in the clothing at the waist could forewarn of a gun or knife. A stagger observed could indicate an illness or the use of drugs or alcohol. Any of these could spell trouble. The mediator can then take action to correct a situation which might surface in other ways later on if it had not been recognized.

Once the clients have been seated in the mediation room, the mediator will take his seat in such a way so that he can communicate with equal ease to each client and without appearing to show favoritism. This is covered elsewhere in the book. Here, the important aspect of where and how the mediator sits is related to his safety. The mediator should sit in a comfortable position slightly forward in his chair, with both feet flat on the floor. When using a table, the mediator's hands will normally be on the tabletop in front of him. When not using a table, the mediator's hands will rest comfortably on his knees or on the arms of the chair. It is important for the mediator to convey openness and interest through body language. It is also crucial that the mediator be seated and remain seated in a position offering the greatest flexibility to respond to whatever transpires during the session. Expecting the unexpected means being ready and more importantly, being able to respond as needed.

Fortunately, that sitting position which provides the greatest position of openness and interest also is the safest position from which the mediator can respond. If violence erupts between the parties, the mediator's hands are in front of him and his legs under him so that movement to interrupt or correct the situation can be made instantly. If the parties leave their chairs in anger, either at one another or at the mediator, the mediator can also leave his chair quickly, preventing him from remaining in a compromising position. When the clients are up, the mediator can rise up also. A position that is too relaxed, or one in which the mediator's legs are tangled or crossed may not allow the needed response speed. Hands open or in front of you on the table will allow you to protect yourself if necessary, and also to respond to the hands of your clients should tempers and actions flare.

Approaching the Subject of Weapons with Clients

Do not be shy! Be direct and precise. If you feel that there is a real danger of weapons by either party, or you suspect that weapons are carried on the person or in the belongings of the clients, action must be taken to prevent these from being brought into or used in a mediation session. Often, a premediation caucus can be arranged, with one party to the dispute coming in at a time different than the other party. The issue of weapons can be raised at that time and disposed of without incident. Mediator concerns about weapons couched in the mediator's real concern about the safety of all concerned will get the message across to the parties. If weapons have been part of the dispute prior to the parties coming for mediation, this fact can be used as an explanation of why the mediator is approaching the subject with each client. If the presence of weapons is based on a hunch or indirect indications picked up by the mediator, the question of weapons should be asked directly. Clients should also be told that no weapons of any kind are permitted in any mediation session, and that the client possessing a weapon must surrender it, leave it at home or at least locked in the trunk of his car prior to any attempt at mediation. Refusal to comply or to satisfy the mediator that weapons are not present, or at least have been disposed of, will result in the refusal of the mediator to begin the session.

Weapons Affidavit

The use of a weapons affidavit executed by each party separately is advised in cases where weapons are suspected or actually present. An example of such an affidavit is shown in Figure 48. The use of a weapons affidavit cannot in itself insure that no weapons are present, but combined with the other measures outlined, can be an effective tool. After explaining the concern of the agency and your concern about the possibility of weapons in the session, explain further that it is agency policy in such matters that a weapons affidavit be executed. As a rule, an affidavit of this nature will not be part of every client's folder. For that reason, the mediator must know where these forms are located and when they should be used. The signing of the weapons affidavit serves as a psychological deterrent to the presence of weapons also. The document itself looks imposing and requires the names and signatures of both parties. It seems to bear out well that those agreements to which a person attaches his signature as a form of commitment are more likely to be adhered to. This is obviously why written agreements rather than oral agreements are suggested and even required when a settlement is reached in mediation. Get the affidavit signed in your presence and let the party see you sign the form as a witness. This will further enhance the strength of the procedure.

WEAPONS AFFIDAVIT

MEDIATION SERVICE OF ANYWHERE, INC.

WEAPONS AFFIDAVIT

I, _____, hereby acknowledge and affirm that any and all weapons possessed by me are not on my person. Further, I hereby release the Dispute Mediation Service from any and all responsibility for any and all violent acts arising out of the behavior of individuals not in its employ in the event of harm to myself and my children (if any), and to those who appear in my behalf.

Signed this _____ day of _____, 19 _____

_____   _____

Witness _____   Date: _____

Figure 48

Weapons and Personal Searches

When a weapons affidavit is introduced, most clients are probably going to be quite willing to prove to you that they possess no weapons. This is so in an attempt to prove to the mediator that any concern about weapons emanates from the other party and not from them. For that reason, actual searches for weapons or of personal belongings should not be approached with timidity by the mediator. However, the mediator must observe certain personal safeguards. Avoid going through someone else's clothing, handbag, packages, and the like. Ask that the client show the mediator through the items in question. A client can open a handbag or package so that the mediator can see the contents. This approach prevents undue liability for the mediator. Pockets can be emptied by the client or the mediator may want to check this area either from the outside or by putting his hands into them. This should be done only with the permission of the client. Often a client will open a jacket, show his pockets, turn around so that the mediator can view his clothing from different angles or otherwise demonstrate that there is no reason to suspect weapons are present. Allow all such demonstrations as they serve a purpose. Be thorough in searching a client if this procedure is necessary. The mediator would not request a search if there were not some concern for his well-being or that of the clients.

If the clients carry articles which may resist easy search, have these items placed outside the mediation room, checked with the receptionist, or at least placed in the far corner of the mediation room to avoid easy access. These items include, but are not limited to, large bags, large purses, heavy coats or packages which are not easily opened. Should anyone refuse to submit to such inquiries or to a search should one be deemed necessary, consideration should be given by the mediator to aborting the mediation effort. Exceptions can be made here, but are done so at the mediator's discretion or after consultation with the agency director or immediate supervisor. Refusal to sign the weapons affidavit will usually be a clue that the mediator's suspicion about weapons was accurate. However, this will not always be the case. Consideration of other factors which might produce such a response must be reviewed. These include the psychological consideration of the client, cultural background, and language barriers to understanding what is being suggested. When such a determination is made, the mediator can decide the proper and most efficient course of action.

If discovered, weapons are surrendered to the mediator, they should be taken from the mediation room and deposited in a prearranged manner with a suitable custodian within the agency. This could be the receptionist or secretary. The procedure for this should be well established with the agency director and all involved need to know what to do to avoid surprises. Some knowledge of weapons and their capabilities, as well as unloading techniques in the case of handguns, rifles and the like will be helpful for all to know. Such training can be arranged locally or through national training agencies. The weapons should be placed in suitable containers, such as a paper bag, or box, and then placed in a locked container for additional safety. Should the weapon not be retrieved after the conclusion of mediation, it can be turned over to a local police agency at a later time. If the owner of the weapon wants it back, it will be returned only after being unloaded. The unloading, in the case of a handgun or rifle, should be done immediately upon voluntary surrender by the client, and then not reloaded again until it has left the agency. It would be well to avoid returning the weapon to a client in the presence of the other party to the dispute. This will avoid post mediation confrontations and additional problems which can impact all concerned.

It should also be noted that if encounters with weapons cannot be handled in the ways described or adapted from what has been described, that local law enforcement officials should be summoned to assist. While probably unnecessary in most cases, this assistance should not be ignored when needed, and indeed will do little to adversely affect an already aborted mediation attempt.

The Mediator's Safety Checklist

1. Do not take the possibility of weapons lightly.
2. Plan in advance for your personal safety and the safety of your clients.
3. Check the arrangement of your office or mediation room. Be sure that all safety factors are accounted for before beginning a mediation session.
4. When greeting your clients, notice anything strange or unusual about their words, actions or dress. Train yourself to pick up on their "vibes" and to learn to understand what they may mean.
5. Learn to read body language.
6. Avoid having your back to your clients, especially those whom you suspect may erupt violently, or who may have weapons.
7. Enter the mediation room behind your clients.
8. Have your clients sit with their backs in the direction of the door through which they will go when they leave.
9. Remove any potential weapon from the mediation room and from the table or desk used for mediation prior to bringing in the parties.
10. Seat clients so that the most potentially violent person does not have to pass close to the other party when entering the room.
11. Use your table or desk as a barrier between you and the clients and/or between the clients themselves as needed.
12. Sit in such a manner that you convey openness and interest as well as maintaining the ability to react quickly to outbreaks of violence or to be able to come to standing position should the clients stand.
13. Try to keep the clients seated during the mediation. This is especially true when violence is suspected. It is much harder to take an aggressive stand from a sitting position than from a standing position.
14. Discuss suspected weapons with the client separately from the other party in a direct and precise manner. Avoid euphemisms.
15. Require a weapons affidavit when deemed necessary.
16. Require personal searches when necessary. Check clothing, pockets, purses, bags, packages, coats and the like.
17. Have all weapons surrendered to a weapons custodian or at least locked in the trunk of the client's car.
18. Unload all weapons confiscated, if applicable.
19. Return weapons as requested, or turn them over to a law enforcement agency.
20. Take seriously your safety and the safety of your clients. Refuse to mediate if your concerns about safety are not satisfied.

XII. Dealing with Hostility

Because of the nature of the process, which permits a controlled confrontation between the parties, participants in dispute mediation often experience heightened emotions. These emotions may be related to the simple confines of the immediate dispute, or may have their roots in long-standing bitterness and conflict between the parties. In either case, the mediation session may be the trigger for additional expressions of the feelings which have either been held inside or which have been expressed repeatedly outside the session. Hostility and its expression are realities that must be acknowledged by the mediator, studied carefully, allowed when productive, and guided towards positive ends for both disputants. To enter a mediation session as a mediator without recognition of the possibilities for both expressed and unexpressed hostility and the effects and potentials for such is to enter unprepared, with unrealistic expectations. To assume that any expression of emotion or hostility is to be avoided and not addressed is equally naive and avoidant. Not all expressions of hostile feelings are counterproductive. Neither is the absence of hostility always productive. The mediator has the responsibility of assessing the levels of feeling which exist and of dealing with them in ways which enhance the mediation attempt, prevent unwanted and non-productive escalation, and protect those who may become inadvertent victims of unprovoked hostile actions or expressions.

The best resources that the mediator has in assessing hostility levels in disputants both before and during the mediation is his experience and attention. Nothing seems to work better in picking up indications of hostile feelings than the sensing mechanisms of the human body. However, their usefulness is limited by the willingness of the mediator to learn to understand what is being sensed, and how to interpret these messages in a way that will protect the mediator and the disputants. The mediator must learn not to ignore information which he obtains in this way. Physical and subcortical awareness may precede cortical awareness and understanding of exactly what is going on. Nevertheless, information obtained in this way and stored as hunches or suspicions can provide the basis for more complete understanding as the case unfolds. The pre-warning of what is to come, even though not clear, can keep the mediator from being surprised when emotions surface during mediation.

Expressions of hostility, in themselves, do not mean that mediation of a dispute is not possible or that a mediation session must be aborted. Such times do exist, but more often hostility can be acknowledged, examined, allowed, redirected and even used to gain a better settlement. In any event, the mediator must remain in control of a mediation session in which there is great hostility, just as the mediator must control sessions in which hostility is a minor concern. Control, coupled with mediator awareness, can be the key to effective hostility diffusion and utilization. If the mediator is intimidated by clients who may be upset with each other, the mediator, the system or with other hidden agendae, and if he is unprepared for an eruption, any opportunity for mediation may be lost. Once lost, it may not be possible to regain the needed momentum and credibility to begin again.

Assessing the emotional level of the client begins when the mediator first meets the parties to the dispute. A simple handshake, eye contact, side comments, or sarcastic remarks are a few of the possible clues that suppressed feelings may exist. If such suppression is occurring, expression may also occur, given opportunity and occasion. Once in the session, the conduct of the parties may give additional clues. How each enters the room, how the chair is pulled from the table, how each takes his seat and begins to get ready for the session are all communications. If a great deal of hostility or potential hostility is detected on initial contact, seat the parties so that they do not have to pass one another when entering the mediation room or going to their seat. This will avoid providing a trigger for hostile expressions or hostile actions toward either party. It is often helpful to let the party who seems the most upset begin the mediation. Doing this allows for immediate ventilation which may otherwise preclude resolution. Because anger and hostility are real to the parties experiencing them, they must be acknowledged, and acknowledged in a way that permits the angry party to know he is understood. The mediator cannot erase the hostility that is felt. However, empathetic reflection can reduce the intensity of the moment. Often a disputant merely wants to be understood and his feelings given credibility. All of us have experienced anger and even rage at some time or other. It is not bad that such feelings are experienced. Neither is the disputant who feels himself wrong for having the experience. All expressions of feeling need to be heard, understood as much as possible, given credibility and utilized constructively.

Within a session, the mediator must demonstrate that he is in total control of the proceedings. Not to do so, especially in the face of hostility or potential hostility, invites immediate ventilation. The mediator must establish the ground rules for mediation, not only what is said, but also how it is said. This will set the tone for the rest of the work to be done. When the mediator takes and maintains control of the session, he also demonstrates clearly that he can and will channel any outbreak of violence or hostility. While hostility demonstrates the presence of great energy which can be redirected for the benefit of the mediation, it must be made clear to the disputants that disruption of the mediation by this same energy will not be allowed. This can be done with direct and succinct statements which respond to indicators of the presence of hostility. Reminding the disputants of your awareness of their feelings and of the purpose of mediation in trying to help them solve their differences will often prove helpful. Caucusing with each party and discussing the positive and negative aspects of their expressions may also serve the ends of your attempts to mediate.

Direct confrontation produces higher returns than ignoring outbursts by either party. The feelings will not vanish. They will continue, and if permitted to escalate, will sabotage even the best efforts at settlement. Dealing with hostility at its first expression will usually prove more beneficial than postponing such an encounter. Ground rules, empathy, clearly stated expectations of behavior by the mediator, caucusing and obvious control by the mediator can and will make a difference in such situations. Throughout the sessions, seek ways in which the experienced feelings of the disputants can be rerouted for their benefit. Such energy can be used in a positive way if the disputant can see that his needs will be more nearly quickly satisfied if emotions are controlled. How this can be shown to a disputant will vary with the person, his needs, and of course the situation. As the mediator feels more and more comfortable handling strong expressions of feelings in the mediation sessions, he will develop greater skill in redirecting their expression.

There may be times in which the hostility felt by either or both disputants or expressed by them in the session may preclude continuation of the mediation attempt. If such is the case, the mediator must be sensitive to such an occurrence and continue to exercise control in terminating the session. How the session is terminated is important for many reasons. The expressions of hostility which lead to the termination of the session may continue after the session is terminated, with serious results. While the mediator is not responsible for what happens outside the sessions, he can take precautions which may reduce the likelihood of serious consequences after the session and may provide options to again attempt mediation with the same disputants in the future. If the session must be terminated, it must be terminated by the mediator rather than by the disputants. It may be their hostility, but it is the mediator's control, choice and decision to end a session. In ending a session, the mediator will state clearly that he is ending the session because of the refusal of the party or parties to continue in a constructive manner conducive to settlement. This statement in itself may be enough to redirect the behavior of the disputants. However, if such is not the case, the session must be ended for that time period. At that point, the mediator may exercise any number of options available to him.

Sending the parties out of the session one at a time, and allowing time for complete departure may be advantageous in preventing precipitous actions in the reception area or in the parking lot. Caucusing with each party in an attempt to see if each is desirous of attempting to continue the mediation at another time may clarify their real intentions. Caucusing can also be used to allow either or both of the parties to fully ventilate before leaving the mediation center or agency, thereby further reducing the potential for subsequent flareups, even though mediation may not be possible at that time.

Extreme threats of violence or hostility, while rare, must be met with previously developed precautions to protect all concerned. Arrangements with local law enforcement authorities can be made prior to these types of occurrences. Standard operating procedures can be maintained between the mediation center or agency and such emergency response groups so that should the need arise, all will understand what is happening and what is needed immediately. In addition to law enforcement groups, paramedical agencies and the like can be contacted and contingency plans developed.

Response to violence can take many forms with variable results, depending on the response posture taken. Mediator safety is paramount in priority assignments. The first job of the mediator in dealing with hostile or potentially hostile situations is not to get hurt. Other priorities are the disputants, their family, other mediators, receptionists and the like. But first, the mediator. If the mediator subjects himself to unnecessary and unneeded risks which result in personal injury, the mediator ceases to be a source of help to the disputants. The mediator cannot continue to function effectively if his personal jeopardy is involved. Risk is part of the job; jeopardy is not. Riskmanship may mean making calculated judgments about action to be taken. It does not mean subjecting oneself to situations in which the threat of personal injury is a certainty.

For these reasons, part of the mediator's job in handling hostility is sensing when to continue to deal with expressions of anger, rage and the like, and when to call it quits and get out. Knowing how and when to get out of a situation is just as important in mediation as knowing how and when to get involved in a dispute. Again, the sensing mechanisms of the mediator provide the best information about impending danger in a session. The mediator must continually interpret his feelings and the feelings of the disputants. Remaining in a bad situation against your own intuition is not good mediation any more than panic because of poorly developed skills is helpful to anyone involved. Recognition, training, knowledge and experience as well as willingness on the part of the mediator to continue to refine his or her skills will more often than not leave all alive. Expressions of hostility are not to be feared. They must be understood, examined and redirected as much as possible. Such expressions must also be respected for their potential and preparation made for effective action to forestall danger and injury if the eventuality should present itself.

Guidelines for Understanding and Handling Hostility Or Hostile Gestures

1. Handle the problems of hostility by preventing them from happening in the first place.
2. Handle physical violence by immediate separation of the parties.
3. Learn to attend to one's own senses in determining impending crisis in a mediation session.
4. Remain in firm control at all times.
5. Take action. All action must be warranted, effective, clear and knowledgeable.
6. Pay attention to the physical arrangement of the mediation room to provide the best alternatives for handling hostility.
7. Enforce ground rules firmly.
8. Allow the expressions of hostile feelings in a mediation session.
9. Be aware at all times of the potential for violence and hostility in a mediation session.
10. Convey control, concern, sensitivity, effectiveness, warmth and integrity in posture, verbal presentations, and physical and psychological attitudes.
11. Demonstrate that the hostility of one client will be handled without intercession of the other client.
12. Terminate the mediation session at the point when it becomes clear that progress is no longer possible because of hostility or potentially hostile actions. This is done to salvage the possibility of future negotiations.
13. Use firmness in the face of hostility.
14. Realize that hostility can be a sign of impending crisis in the life of the disputant.
15. Recognize and confront hostile body language in a disputant constructively.
16. Prevent guns, knives and other weapons from being brought into the mediation session and causing injury. (See chapter on Safety and Weapons)
17. Provide for the security of mediation offices and agencies, and establish standard operating procedures with law enforcement and paramedical agencies.
18. Consider a "buddy system" for mediators to enable them to respond to and assist each other when needed. This is especially important whenever mediation takes place after usual business hours or when the building is closed.
19. Provide clear explanations of security arrangements in potentially volatile situations to curtail future problems.
20. It has been said that in situations of hostility or violence, there is no such thing as a fair fight. Prepare yourself with skills, protective measures, knowledge and back-up support in advance. Do not be hesitant to use them.

XIII. Special Problems in Mediation

Empowering

Power in mediation can come from several sources. Certainly the power that each disputant feels that he has is very real to him even though it may not stand the test of negotiation or of law. Power can also be seen in the way the mediator conducts the session and maintains his own psychological posture throughout. Power can also be implied through threats and evidence of one disputant to or against the other. Power comes in many forms, but one thing seems clear: power is a factor that must be understood by the mediator so that he can direct, equalize, utilize and scrutinize it during the mediation. Not to understand the role and presence of power is to avoid an entire area of major consequence in the final outcome of negotiations.

Each party to a mediation, including the mediator, wants to feel that he has power over his life and certainly over the mediation. For that reason, clashes between the power of the mediator and the power of either disputant must be examined. If the parties to the dispute are led to believe that each is powerless as contrasted to the all-wielding power of the mediator, each may be less likely to invest himself in the process. However, they must be helped to see that although the mediator sets the basic procedure for mediation and exercises control in this way, that the real exercise of power and direction over the dispute rests with each of the parties involved. This can be done effectively by their recognizing that a dispute and its problems belongs to the disputants, and that what they do to resolve the situation is up to them, and to them alone. The mediator's power becomes effective in placing responsibility squarely where it belongs; on the shoulders of the disputants. The mediator empowers the parties by refusing to accept the responsibility for solving their problems. In the same sense, the mediator does not act as the judge in the legal system with which they may be familiar. He becomes the agent for placing the burden of the problem as well as the power for problem solving with those who can in reality do the best job of doing what needs to be done.

Inequality of power often exists between the parties to a dispute because of differences in experience, knowledge, skills or position. A dispute between a father and child, an employer and employee, husband and wife, a highly verbal person and a less verbal opponent, or someone of above average intellectual functioning and of barely average ability, are all examples often seen in mediation of power inequalities. Often it is the more powerful party who initiates the mediation, perhaps in an attempt to utilize this power to the greatest advantage possible, knowing that the other party cannot compete as well in such a situation. Conversely, a weaker party may initiate a mediation in order to gain additional power from the mediator or from the process itself. In any case, successful mediation cannot occur between unequals. One party to a dispute cannot be expected to take full responsibility for settlement if he is constantly operating from a position of weakness relative to the other party. In such cases, bullying may occur and the agreement reached put in jeopardy for a great many seemingly obvious reasons. Conversely, those who feel that they had a meaningful part in arriving at settlement are more likely to perform under the contract.

Because mediation relies so heavily on good faith, even with the presence of a signed and enforceable contract, every attempt must be made to make each disputant the owner of the dispute and of the power of its settlement.

The question of how to equalize power in obviously unequal circumstances must be addressed in such a way as to allow the mediator to realize his responsibility in the equalization process while at the same time not overstepping the bounds of problem ownership. Effective mediation ceases at either extreme. Unequal parties cannot mediate effectively, nor can mediation continue if the mediator has assumed responsibility for either or both disputants.

Bringing about the equalization of power depends on several factors. Among these are the degree of disparity in power levels in the parties, the ability of the disputants to assume power, and the skill of the mediator in performing equalizing actions. Simple techniques such as furniture arrangement in the mediation room or seating one disputant before the other may affect equalization and stabilization of power. Bringing the disputant perceived to have less power into the room first and placing him in what might be seen as a more commanding position at the mediation table may serve to equalize the power disparity when the second party is brought into the room. A more involved way of dealing with power inequalities may be to insist that all parties to a dispute investigate all aspects of the items to be mediated prior to commencement of negotiations. The example here is a divorcing couple attempting to use mediation as a means of handling the divorce. If the husband appears to be extremely knowledgeable of his rights, financial situation, and property, while the wife has never learned about such things, a trip to an attorney may be a necessary recommendation to make to the wife prior to attempting the mediation.

Caucusing is another way to deal with inequalities of power. The disputant with the apparent greater power can be helped to explore the results of overplaying that strength, while the less empowered disputant can be helped to explore alternatives which clearly demonstrate that he is not as powerless as previously thought. The employer, for example, who feels that he "holds all the aces" in a dispute with a fired employee, can be assisted to look at the future ramifications of dealing unfairly with an employee. Those ramifications can include bad press for the company, word of mouth insinuations and the development of unions where none currently exist. The employee might be directed to find other ways of approaching the conflict should mediation fail, while at the same time being shown that there are ways to approach the employer to encourage a better chance of settlement. How to prepare a proposal to the employer and how to use a "fall-back" position can also be explored.

Costing can also be used as a way to show the power of each party. Even the disputant who feels that if he does not get what he wants can take the other party to court can see the time and financial output necessary to such action. Additionally, the right of the other party to file countersuits can also add to power that can be utilized should mediation fail. Seeing that the opponent has more power than originally thought can be not only an equalizer in mediation, but also a reason to participate fully in the process to avoid adversarial litigation.

Maintaining the balance of power in mediation is an important aspect of the mediator's role. This must be done while at the same time exercising the mediator's power to the extent necessary to enable the process to continue. How the mediator does this will be different for different mediators. One thing seems clear, however. The way in which the mediator approaches the session, his mental attitude, the understanding of the place of power in mediation, physical bearing and skill in equalizing power will be crucial aspects of the mediator's interpersonal involvement.

Mediation and Individual Capacity

Differences which normally exist in people affect their ability to enter successfully into mediation. Mediation requires a certain verbal facility. Therefore, clients with below average skills in this area will be less able to negotiate; not because they might not want to, but because they cannot. Physical disabilities, brain dysfunctions or damage and the like may also contribute to an individual difference which would make mediation impossible. The mediator must be aware that such things adversely affect ability and may not be within the control of the party.

Far more important than the developmental, intellectual or impairment differences which affect mediation are the differences brought about by the willingness or unwillingness of the disputants to enter into mediation. Not all persons who come to the mediation center are there because they want to negotiate and settle an issue through mediation. Just as people are different, so are their agendae when they come either as the initiating or responding party. The purpose of one may be quite different than that of the other, even though both appear ostensibly to settle an issue. Recognition of the differences in agendae is crucial if the mediator is to avoid spending time and effort at mediation only to have it sabotaged because of an unwillingness to participate on the part of one or both parties.

Clarification by the mediator early in the session of the reasons for each disputant's participation and his desire to settle can save problems and eliminate later frustration. If the disputants are unwilling to give clear answers that demonstrate their willingness to enter into mediation and move toward settlement, the mediator should move no further until such commitment is gained. Without a clear commitment from the disputants, even the most skilled mediator can hope for little more than a session which will be eventually aborted. The disputant's responses to questions about his reasons for seeking mediation will also reveal whether there is an ego-involvement in settling the dispute. Usually, asking each disputant what has brought him to mediation and if he would be willing to enter into a signed agreement if one is reached will give some indication as to individual intent. Clear yes or no responses to the mediator's questions in those areas should be elicited. Often one disputant will respond to such questioning by telling those present that he is there to "see what happens," because he can always take the other party to court. In such cases, asking what has prevented the disputant from already doing that will expose the more immediate reasons for seeking mediation rather than legal alternatives. Unless both parties are willing to enter into negotiations in such a way that will allow movement toward the goal of consensual settlement, it may be better to terminate the session until such time as willingness is evidenced.

Mediating Life Passages

Mediation is the process by which parties to a dispute are helped by a neutral third party to come to consensual settlement of a dispute. Such a definition is often seen to apply to only certain types of disputes. Labor mediation and arbitration are widely known. Recently, non-labor dispute mediation has come into vogue as a real alternative to litigation and adversarial encounter in a court of law. Even divorce mediation has made its debut as a viable alternative to lengthy and expensive court battles over custody, property, visitation and the like. Even with all its proliferation, mediation is sometimes seen in a very limited way rather than the way of the future for settling almost any kind of dispute. If a dispute can be caused by humans, what would prevent those same humans from settling the problem together? Such an approach requires public education about the value of the mediation process. One sure thing is that engaging in legal battles

Mediation Along the Family Life Cycle

Pre-Marital Mediation
Mediators are helping couples draw up marriage agreements prior to the ceremony. This "ounce of prevention" can help to insure a more stable marriage.

Disabled and Handicapped
Stress often occurs in families caring for disabled or handicapped members. Counselors are using mediation to resolve some of the resulting conflicts.

Teenage Pregnancy
Struggles often arise over situations involving unmarried pregnant teenagers. Mediation can assist in resolving the conflicts between the parents and child.

Homosexuals
Gay couples ending a relationship often have many of the same conflicts that married couples do when they divorce. The legal system does not necessarily provide a forum for their disputes, so mediation can be valuable in resolving disputes over child custody, joint real estate ventures, and future support payments.

Unmarried Cohabitants
At least one campus mediation service handles disputes between non-married couples who live together and seek a solution other than separation.

Figure 49. (Reprinted with permission. From the *Futurist,* February 1982 by Patricia Vroom, Diane Fassett and Rowan Wakefield.)

Teenagers and Parents
Numerous conflicts arise between parents and their adolescent children. Parent-teenager disputes often involve power struggles, and mediation can help restore relative peace to these households.

Runaways
Mediation is being used to bring together runaways and their families, and to resolve their conflicts out of court. Mediators are also helping to resolve family differences caused by juvenile drug abusers.

Relocation
New comprehensive relocation services use mediation to resolve the conflicts brought to the surface by a family move, such as problems related to dual careers, care of dependents, adolescent anxieties, and general emotional problems.

Domestic Violence
Mediation is helpful in the area of spouse abuse, particularly with first-time abusers.

Separation and Divorce
Property settlements and support payments are often the two areas of greatest contention in separation and divorce disputes. Mediation helps the couple to separate emotional issues from financial decisions.

Custody and Visitation
Mediation allows for more flexible and finely tailored child custody arrangements than those resulting from the adversarial process. Couples often reach cooperative joint custody agreements.

Retirement
Mediation services can help settle disputes at retirement time, such as when a husband might want to move to Florida just when his wife is embarking on a new career.

The Elderly vs. Their Middle-Aged Children
With the elderly population increasing, more and more conflicts are arising when older people can no longer care for themselves. Mediators help families to reach decisions about institutional versus home care.

Wills and Estate Planning
Mediation is useful when families disagree over estate plans. It also cuts costs when family members are contesting the execution of a relative's will.

has become so costly in our society that many people are looking for alternative ways of settling their differences. Mediation is that alternative. When properly used, it provides for neutral assistance in settling disputes arising from almost any area of the life cycle through which we all must pass. (See figure 49).

Couples contemplating marriage may find that premarital mediation can assist them to handle many problems prior to marriage which might cause difficulty later. Premarriage agreements which help to add structure to the beginning of a relationship may add stability not otherwise present. The agreement may also help to set the pattern of face to face negotiations which may aid the marriage in subsequent years.

Unmarried persons of opposite sex who share living space may benefit from mediation. Disputes arising from such a relationship, if successfully mediated, may negate the need for dissolution of the relationship and/or living arrangement. Homosexual couples may also gain relief from disputes arising in much the same way as those with married/unmarried couples. The court system provides much less remedy for this type of relationship, yet such a relationship may need assistance both during and after dissolution as does a heterosexual one. Custody, visitation, support, property are all very real concerns in all such intimate relationships and mediation offers the possibility of healthy settlement.

Within heterosexual marriages, mediation is invaluable in settling disputes arising from difficulties with children, teenage pregnancies, runaways, spouse abuse, teenage problems and separation and divorce. Struggles commonly occurring between parents and their children as well as those involving unwanted pregnancies, drug abuse, power struggles, runaways and the like can be dealt with through the use of a neutral third party intervener. In so doing, not only can families learn to work together to solve problems of mutual concern and thereby avoid problems inherent in the legal system, but also teach children that problems can be handled by the parties involved in an intelligent and civil way. Even some cases of spouse abuse can be handled though mediation if there is a desire by both parties to recognize the problems and seek meaningful solutions.

Separation and divorce of married couples can be handled through mediation in such a way as to save not only the divorcing parties, but also the children involved, from unnecessary pain and suffering which often accompanies more traditional attempts at these matters. Mediation allows the couple to make its own decisions about what is best for both themselves and those who are closest to them. One major advantage is the cost of the mediative process when compared with the cost of adversarial divorce. Cost is not only measured in terms of dollars, but also in terms of suffering and scarring for all participants. Living arrangements, visitation, support, joint involvement in the rearing and growth of the child and all related financial issues can be settled by the parties themselves.

Another life cycle event which may cause conflict is family relocation due to job change or other unforeseen circumstances. Mediation is helpful here and is sometimes used by relocation agencies to help minimize the conflict brought to the surface in such circumstances.

As the cycle of life continues, problems and disputes occur between older children and their aging parents. Disabled adults living in a household may also be the source of conflict which may be resolved through mediation. Even retirement and the problems often associated with it can be dealt with. Husbands and wives may experience difficulty in making decisions about how to spend retired years and the neutral third party mediator can assist them to generate meaningful alternatives. The disputes that may arise between older adults and their children who want to place them in retirement homes may be helped with mediation. Alternatives can be explored and ways of strengthening this important relationship can be developed. Without such help, important ties become frayed and even broken between persons who profess much caring and love for one another.

The life cycle ends for all intents and purposes with death. Mediation can help families with estate planning, execution of those plans after the passing of family members and even in the less costly execution of the deceased's will. Contests can be avoided and families may avoid the terrible agony that may result from infighting and bickering. When a problem is faced by the parties intimately involved in the conflict, the process of examining the problem changes it. Where there is a commitment to finding a way to solve the problem, regardless of its nature, those so committed can effectively accomplish this. The neutral third party provides the needed structure and assists the parties to generate meaningful alternatives. Throughout life, there are few problems known to man that cannot be solved by man. The only prerequisities are understanding and willingness.

Reference

Vroom, Patricia, Passett, Diane and Wakefield, Rowan, "Winning through Mediation," *The Futurist*, February, 1982.

XIV. Training Needs— A Proposal

One key to successful mediation is thoughtful, well-presented training. While this book is useful to the mediator, it is not a substitute for training. Few standards exist by which to evaluate training programs. This section provides a detailed curriculum and justification of each part of such a program, and is offered as a standard by which proposals may be evaluated. The program contained here is a complete 40-hour program, which is the minimum amount of time recommended. Inquiries regarding training by the authors may be addressed to the publishers of this book.

Program Description

The proposed training program will be almost equally divided between didactic lecture format and experiential learning. While the program will encourage advance preparation for the training experience, the lectures will include materials already presented in the readings, and the readings themselves will be ancillary to the general curriculum, rather than preparation for the training experience. The training will then constitute a second presentation of the written material, plus interpretation of the readings, exercises, demonstrations and simulation.

The training program is more easily divided into time frames than into conceptual areas or divisions between experimentation and lecture. Nevertheless, the following topical outline with approximate time allocations will indicate the proposed subject matter:

Topical Outline of Lectures

1. Definitions: What Is Conflict, Sources of Conflict in Interpersonal Relations?
2. The Psychology of Anger and Conflict
3. Theories of Conflict Management
4. Cognition and Communication: What We Think and Why
5. Cultural Differences and Non-Verbal Communication
6. What is Mediation? Differentiated from:
   Crisis Intervention
   Legal Counseling
   Psychological Counseling
   Negotiation
7. What is a Mediator and What Does the Mediator Do?
8. What is Settlement and What is a Contract?
9. Writing Agreements
10. Dynamics of Settlement in Differing Types of Cases
11. Avoiding the Imposition of Standards by the Mediator

12. The Ethical Dimensions of Mediation
13. The Special Use of Caucusing
14. The Use of Questioning: The Mediator as an Agent of Reality
15. Active Listening: Empathy, Not Sympathy
16. The Process of Mediation
    A. Preparing the Parties
    B. Doing Your Homework
    C. The Physical Environment
    D. The Three Goals of Mediation
        1. Controlling the Argument
        2. Establishing Wants and Needs
        3. Generating Alternatives
    E. The Concept of Process in Mediation
    F. The Initiator's Position:
        1. What to Listen For
        2. Traps of the Injured Party
    G. The Respondent's Position
        1. Legalisms to Avoid
        2. I am Innocent
    H. Establishing the Issues
    I. The Caucus
    J. Breaking Deadlocks
    K. Joint-Costing and Establishing the Need to Settle
    L. Writing the Agreement
    M. The Future of the Profession of Conflict Management
17. The Uses and Methodology of Conciliation

Outline of Experiential Learning

Each lecture topic will be followed immediately by an exercise that is designed to illustrate the major points made in that lecture. All lectures will be limited to 30 minutes and all exercise periods also limited to 30 minutes, except for special topics in conciliation, writing the agreement and the mediation process. Each of these areas has been selected for concentration since they are often the most difficult skills to obtain.

Detailed Curriculum

The entire curriculum is organized by the three tasks which every mediator undertakes when engaging in conflict regulation: managing the argument, differentiating between needs and wants, or establishing the issues, and generating alternatives from which the parties can select their own resolutions. Each topic of lecture and experience falls into one of these concept areas.

Managing the Argument

Management may be defined as the movement of people over time in the service of an idea. Conflict management restrains the destructive impulses to fight and channels them into the task of settlement within the limited time frame of the mediation session. The sub-topics contained within this subject area include: (L indicates lecture, E designates exercise.)

30 minutes—1.	What is Conflict, Sources of Conflict (L)
30 minutes—1a.	Finding your own "hot" button. (E)
30 minutes—2.	Theories of Conflict Management (L)
30 minutes—2a.	Finding Strategies of Conflict (E)
30 minutes—3.	Cognition and Communication (L)
30 minutes—3a.	How We Think and What We Say (E)
30 minutes—4.	Physiology of Anger/Conflict (L)
30 minutes—4a.	Hassle Lines and Escapes (E)
30 minutes—5.	What Mediation Is and What It Isn't (L)
30 minutes—5a.	Experience Counseling, Legal Advice and Crisis Intervention (E)
30 minutes—6.	The Setting, The Parties, The Introduction (L)
30 minutes—6a.	Practice the Process

Differentiating Needs and Wants

The distance between what the parties want and what the parties need is often called the negotiating distance. This distance is the most critical discovery in the mediation process. Without this discovery, the construction of a viable settlement is impossible. If the mediator attends only to the ostensible issues between the parties, any agreement that is reached will be based on convenience, not conviction.

The principal tool in the discovery of this distance is questioning. Questioning is a complex process which involves special skills in listening to both the substantive and affective facts, focusing, and gradual accumulation of points of common agreement. The mediator here becomes an active listener, though still neutral. He negotiates with both sides to discover the real needs and the true position regarding the argument of each. Then he tests all propositions against the desires of the respective sides.

The subtopics contained within this subject area include:

30 minutes—1.	The Use of Questioning—The Mediator as an Agent of Reality (L)
30 minutes—1a.	Four Puzzles Assembled Through Questioning (E)
30 minutes—2.	Cross-Cultural Differences and Non-Verbal Communication (L)
30 minutes—2a.	Exercise in Interpretation of Non-Verbal and Cross Cultural Cues (E)
30 minutes—3.	The Special Use of Caucusing (L)
30 minutes—3a.	Using the Caucus in Three Exemplary Cases (E)
30 minutes—4.	Negotiation and Its Relationship to Mediation (L)
30 minutes—4a.	Competitive vs. Collaborative Games (E)

30 minutes—5.	The Initiator's Position (Traps of the Injured Party, The Respondent) Position, Innocence and Legalisms (L)
30 minutes—5a.	Role Play; Both Initiator and Respondent (E)
30 minutes—6.	Joint Costing and Establishing the Desire to Settle/Active Listening, Empathy Not Sympathy (L)
30 minutes—6a.	Practice on Joint Costing—3 Case Studies (E)
30 minutes—7.	Breaking Deadlocks: The Concept of Stalemate (L)
30 minutes—7a.	Breaking Deadlocks in Three Cases (E)

Generating Alternatives and Creating Agreements

After the conflict has been managed and the needs and wants of the conflicting parties identified, the next crucial phase of the mediation begins: generating alternatives and constructing the agreement. The cliche that most parties need to adopt a win-win solution to their problem is insufficient by itself to compel them to that conclusion. The mediator must have broken the conflict down into the smallest divisible parts and then reassembled them in a series of patterns not unlike a gallery of kaleidoscopic prints. From this large gallery, the conflicting parties are able to select portions of the final portrait. The mediator takes those selections and recombines them in a new picture acceptable to both parties.

This generation of alternatives is necessary because the parties have taken positions from which they find it very difficult to retreat. They are invested in particular patterns of thought that lead inevitably to a predictable conclusion. Yet, by rearranging the patterns of thought and offering scenarios of possible futures, the mediator is able to urge the parties to rethink those patterns.

While each stage of the mediation process is vitally important, the forging of agreement is of special significance. Here, the terms of performance between the parties are reduced to writing. Since it was often the oral, inspecific and presumed agreement that brought the parties to conflict in the first place, the clear, specific and definite recitation of settlement is even more important. Technique becomes vital. Yet, the very highest ethical standards of the mediator will produce clear agreements without coercion and with performance from the parties.

The sub-topics contained within this subject area include:

30 minutes—1.	What is a Settlement Between the Parties? (L)
30 minutes—1a.	Identify the Substantive and Non-Substantive Issues In This Simulation (E)
30 minutes—2.	What is A Contract? (L)
30 minutes—2a.	Practice in Writing a Contract from Three Simulations (E)
30 minutes—3.	The Uses and Methodology of Conciliation (L)
30 minutes—3a.	Practice in Conciliation from Three Simulations (E)
30 minutes—4.	The Dynamics of Different Cases (L)
30 minutes—4a.	Simulations of Settlement in Domestic Relations and Criminal Cases (E)
30 minutes—5.	Avoiding the Imposition of Standards by the Mediator (L)
30 minutes—5a.	Simulations of Difficult Ethical Choices (E)

Simulated Mediations with Critique

The training program should culminate with simulated mediation sessions. These sessions should involve each participant first as an observer, in which the parties observe a prototypic mediation with professional mediators. Next, the participants should act out the role of an initiating party or complainant. Finally, the participant becomes the respondent, the accused wrongdoer. The role play is repeated with three different cases. Therefore, the participant has participated in three cases and has observed one case through settlement.

Ideally, each simulation will be alloted one hour. During fifty minutes of the hour, the participants will attempt to find a resolution to the conflict. During the remaining ten minutes, a detailed critique will be provided by a trained mediator who will have observed the entire mediation session.

At the conclusion of the three critiques provided by the trained mediators, each participant should be given a score sheet on his performance which is intended to highlight strengths and weaknesses and assist the trainee to develop further. Here is a sample agenda.

Simulation Time		Simulaton Topics
50 minutes	1.	Commercial Relations—The Car
10 minutes	1a.	Critique of Performance
50 minutes	2.	Neighborhood Conflict—The Barking Dog
10 minutes	2a.	Critique of Performance
50 minutes	3.	Landlord/Tenant Dispute—I Need More Time
10 minutes	3a.	Critique of Performance
50 minutes	4.	Domestic Relations Dispute, Trainer Conducted for Group Review
10 minutes	4a.	Group Critique and Questions

Specialty Time

In every training program time is consumed in breaks, lunches, warm-up exercises, introductions and debriefing exercises at the conclusion of the day's activities. It is tempting to regard these activities as extraneous to the learning process. In fact, such sessions are designed to:

1. Create positive bonds between participants.
2. Permit a valuable exchange of information between the trainees and participants on an informal basis.
3. Reduce the tension usually produced during the first few learning sessions and make the participants more receptive to the information being provided.
4. Provide the participants an opportunity to incorporate the information already provided into their active memories.

Addendum: Training the Trainer

An additional option may be preparing people to do training in future programs. Every component of the training program will be in written as well as oral form. The training program will be put in writing, and the future trainers will presumably be in attendance during the training session. Therefore, they will be familiarized with the training process as they proceed through the training and may be able to duplicate it later on, with the help of the written material. Of course, prospective trainers should be carefully selected and should undertake additional studies as directed by the original trainers or experienced mediators.

Each of the seven sections of this sample has been designed to enable future trainers to conduct future training programs for that agency.

Each lecture will be transcribed and the transcription edited. The edited transcription of the training presentation will be typewritten with word-processed accuracy and right-justified print. This will enable the parties to read the final document easily. Likewise, the instructions for each exercise as given by the instructors at the mediation training program will be detailed. These instructions will be included in the training manual for future mediators.

A special section of the training manual should be added only for trainers. This section will state additional purposes for the exercises and for the lectures. A set of study questions will be provided for the exercises to guide the instructors in the administration of the program.

Overview of the Training

Managing the Argument	6.0 hours
Differentiating Needs/Wants	7.5 hours
Generating Alternatives	6.5 hours
Simulated Mediations	4.0 hours
Specialty Time (breaks, lunches, etc.)	11.3 hours
How To Be a Trainer	4.0 hours
Flexibility of Time	1.0 hour

40 Total Hours
Expended

Contents of the Mediation Training Manual

1. Introduction to the Concept of Mediation and to the Use of the Training Manual.
2. Managing the Argument
3. Differentiating Needs and Wants
4. Generating Alternatives
5. Simulated Mediations with Critique
6. Guides for the Trainer/Agendas and Instructions
7. How to Be a Trainer
8. Articles and Bibliography
9. Forms from Dispute Resolution Services
10. Agency Policies
11. Mediator Notebook for Personal Observaton and Notes
12. Detailed Budget
13. Notes on Future Selection of Mediators and Need for Evaluation

The Core component of any mediation program is the mediator force. Composed of individuals, this group always demonstrates individual strengths and weaknesses before, during and after training. During the training, a detailed evaluation of each mediator should be made by trainers.

Each mediator will be evaluated on the three skills around which the training program is designed; taking control of the argument, establishing negotiating distances, and generating alternatives. Additionally, each mediator will be rated according to criteria found predictive of future performances. These criteria include: attentiveness to training, flexibility of approach, verbal facility and potential for future growth.

A Final Word

A sample agenda follows. The agenda is based on the descriptions provided above. It provides a detailed breakdown of the proposal as it would fit into a two-weekend program, starting on a Friday evening and ending on a Sunday evening.

Day 1

Begin/end	Topic	Length
6:00 PM—6:10	Welcome To Training	10 min.
6:10 PM—6:25	Intro. of Trainers	15 min.
6:25 PM—6:55	Explanation of Purposes of Training Program	30 min.
6:55 PM—7:15	Review of Logistics	20 min.
7:15 PM—7:25	EXERCISE: Interview Your Partner. Divide the time equally. Discover all you can.	10 min.
7:25 PM—8:10	Introduce Your Partner. You have 1 minute. Then your partner introduces you.	45 min.
8:10 PM—8:25	Break: Please mingle with someone you have not met.	15 min.
8:25 PM—8:55	Cognition and Communication	30 min.
8:55 PM—9:10	Exercise on Cognition and Communication	15 min.
9:10 PM—9:35	Physiology and communication	25 min.
9:35 PM—9:55	Questions and answers	20 min.
9:55 PM—10:00	Review of next day's activities	5 min.

Day 2

Begin/End	Topic	Length
9:00 AM—9:05 AM	Welcome	5 min.
9:05 AM—9:20 AM	Exercise: Hassle Lines—	15 min.
9:20 AM—9:50 AM	What is Conflict?	30 min.
9:50 AM—10:05AM	Exercise: Finding your Own Button/What Makes You Angry?	15 min.
10:05AM—10:35 AM	Lecture: Theories of Conflict Management	30 min.
10:35 AM—11:00 AM	Break: Mingle with someone new.	25 min.
11:00 AM—11:30 AM	What is Mediation? (vis-a-vis arbitration and law)	30 min.
11:30 AM—12:00 AM	What Mediation Is Not (vis-a-vis counselling and crisis intervention)	30 min.
1:00 PM—1:45 PM	The Setting, the Introduction/ Controlling the Exchanges (including demonstration)	45 min.
1:45 PM—2:15 PM	Practice the Introduction & Process (Simulation #1 in assigned rooms)	30 min.
2:15 PM—2:45 PM	Differentiating Needs and Wants: The Use of Questioning	30 min.
2:45 PM—3:15 PM	Practice the Use of Questioning	30 min.
3:15 PM—3:40 PM	Cultural Differences & Interpreting Non-Verbal Behavior	25 min.
3:40 PM—3:55 PM	Break. Meet someone new.	15 min.
3:55 PM—4:15 PM	EXERCISE: Interpreting Nonverbal Behavior	20 min.
4:15 PM—5:00 PM	Film on Non-Verbal Communications	45 min.
5:00 PM—5:45 PM	The Special Uses of Conciliation	45 min.
5:45 PM—6:00 PM	Questions and Closure	15 min.

The final five minutes of each lecture is designed to receive questions regarding the presentation.

Day 3

Begin/End	Topic	Length
1:00 PM—1:10	Welcome	10 min.
1:10 PM—1:30	Continuing Demonstration: Establishing the Desire to Settle	20 min.
1:30 PM—2:00	Joint Costing to Establish the Desire to Settle/Active Listening Empathy not Sympathy	30 min.
2:00 PM—2:30	Practice on Joint Costing & Establishing the Need to Settle	30 min.
2:30 PM—3:00	Special Use of Caucusing	30 min.
3:00 PM—3:30	Practice the Use of Caucusing	30 min.
3:30 PM—3:45	Break: Meet someone new.	15 min.
3:45 PM—4:15	Breaking Deadlocks Lecture & Demonstration	30 min.
4:15 PM—5:00	Practice the Use of Breaking Deadlocks	45 min.
5:00 PM—5:15	Summary of Weekend Activities	15 min.
5:15 PM—6:00	Questions-Discussion and Review of the Next Weekend	45 min.

Day 4

Begin/End	Topic	Length
6:00 PM—6:20 PM	Welcome	20 min.
6:20 PM—6:50 PM	Continuing Simulation/The Settlement.	30 min.
6:50 PM—7:20 PM	What is a Contract of Settlement Between the Parties	30 min.
7:20 PM—7:40 PM	Break: Meet someone new	20 min.
7:40 PM—8:40 PM	Practice in Writing Contracts by the Mediator Class	60 min.
8:40 PM—9:10 PM	The Dynamics of Settlement in Different Cases	30 min.
9:10 PM—9:50 PM	Three Vignettes: Commercial Relations Employer/Employee and Domestic Rel.	40 min.
9:50 PM—10:00 PM	Questions and Closure	10 min.

Day 5

Begin/End	Topic	Length
9:00 AM—9:10	Welcome	10 min.

9:10 AM—10:30 AM	Replay by Trainers of:
	  a. Introductions
	  b. Use of Questioning
	  c. Controlling Exchanges
	  d. Use of Caucusing
	  e. Joint Costing
	  f. Breaking Deadlocks
	  g. Writing Agreement
		80 min.

10:30—10:45 AM	Break. Meet Someone New.	15 min.
10:45—11:00 AM	Questions on Mediation Process	15 min.
11:00—11:30 AM	Negotiations & Mediation	30 min.
11:30—12:00 Noon	Avoiding the Imposition of Standards by the Mediator	30 min.
1:00—2:00 PM	Mediation Simulation One Report to Mediation Rooms. Last 10 minutes for critique.	60 min.
2:00—3:00 PM	Mediation Simulation Two Report to Mediation Rooms. Last 10 minutes for critique	60 min
3:00—3:15 PM	Break. Meet Someone new.	15 min.
3:15—4:15 PM	Mediation Simulation Three Report to Mediation Rooms. Last 10 minutes for critique	60 min.
4:15—4:30 PM	Debriefing and Questions.	15 min.
4:30—5:10 PM	Evaluations of trainees Ten minutes each	40 min.
5:10—5:30 PM	The Mediator Force and its Management (by host organization)	20 min.
5:30—5:50 PM	Final questions	30 min.
5:50—6:00 PM	Evaluation by trainees	10 min.

Day 6

Begin/End	Topic	Length
1:00 PM—1:10	Welcome	10 min.
1:10 PM—1:40 PM	The Mediation Movement in the U.S.	30 min.
1:40 PM—2:30 PM	Full Mediation Demonstration and Questions	50 min.
2:30 PM—2:45 PM	Break	15 min.
2:45 PM—4:00 PM	Crisis Intervention and Mediation Two Levels of Control and Interaction—Questions	75 min.
4:00 PM—4:45 PM	Ethics Panel—Difficult Ethical Choices for Mediators	45 min.
4:45 PM—5:15 PM	Logistics (by host organization)	30 min.
5:15 PM—5:30 PM	Question Period	15 min.
5:30 PM—6:00 PM	Tour of Facilities (by host org.)	30 min.
6:45 PM	Keynote Address	30 min.
7:15 PM	Presentation of Certificates Oath or Affirmation of Service	15 min.

Conclusion of the first stage of the training program.

Mediator Survival in Crisis Situations

In addition to basic mediator training programs as outlined above, additional training may be necessary to develop skills in the mediator which allow him or her to survive even the most difficult, unusual and often stress producing mediation sessions. Hostility, severe emotional upsets, and threats of violence can occur and be disrupting, if not devastating, to mediation, the mediator, and to the clients. What the mediator does to resolve such situations so that the mediation can continue will determine the ultimate success or failure of the mediation effort.

In response to this special need, training in Crisis Management for mediators has been developed and is designed to teach the novice, as well as the experienced mediator, how to handle such situations. The design was done by those experienced in both mediation and crisis intervention. The one day, eight hour, in-service course is planned in such a way that time is well spent, and is cost effective to almost any agency. Practical, immediately useable information is provided, and each student has the opportunity to develop and to practice skills learned during the training sessions.

The importance of such additional training cannot be overemphasized. If the skills developed save only one mediation, or one life, the additional time spent in this program is well invested. What follows is an example of such a training program as described above, which has been used successfully, both in total and in part, to provide Crisis Intervention training for mediators. Additional information about this program can be obtained by writing the publishers of this book with your specific request.

Training Schedule for One Day (8 hours) Program

SCHEDULE

9 AM	to	9:10	Introduction and welcome
9:10	to	9:20	Review of schedule for the day
9:20	to	10:20	The Mediation: Self Survival, Client Survival, Process Survival Mediation vs. Crisis Intervention
10:20	to	10:30	Break
10:30	to	11:15	Crisis in Mediation—Simulation/Demonstration Crucial relationship of Crisis Intervention to Mediation
11:15	to	12 Noon	Crisis behavior and symptoms What to look for and where to look Awareness as the integral component
12:00	to	1:00	Lunch (working lunch; discussion; questions and answers)
1:00	to	2 PM	Replay and study of mediation simulation Special precautions Safety of the Mediator/Intervener
2:00	to	2:30	Continuation of simulation Questions and Answers
2:30	to	2:45	Break
2:45	to	3:45	Dealing effectively with hostility in mediation Intervention procedures Moving back to "mediation" after "intervention"
3:45	to	4:45	Trainee mediation/crisis situation recreations Critique by self, trainees and trainers
4:45	to	5:00	Questions and Answers Presentation of Certificates
5:00			Adjourn

* This program is designed to be intensive in nature and specific in scope. Students should be prepared for this.
* Each student/trainee should be provided a copy of CRISIS INTERVENTION: A HANDBOOK FOR INTERVENERS by J. Greenstone and S. Leviton prior to the training session and encouraged to read and to study the several chapters on crisis development and Crisis Intervention procedures.

Bibliography

Ardrey, Robert: *Territorial Imperative,* 1966. Dell, New York, New York.

Arendt, Hannah: *Origins of Totalitarianism,* 1966. Harcourt, Brace & World, New York, New York.

Auerbach, Jerold S.: *Justice Without Law?,* 1983. Oxford University Press.

Bandler, Richard and Grinder, John: *The Structure of Magic: A Book about Language and Therapy* (Vol. 1), 1985. Charles Scribner Sons, New York, New York.

Bettleheim, Bruno: *The Informed Heart, Autonomy in a Mass Age,* 1960. Free Press, New York, New York.

Birdwhistell, Ray L.: *Kinesics and Context Essays on Body Motion Communication,* 1970. University of Pennsylvania Press, Philadelphia, Pennsylvania.

Bondurant, Joan: *Conquest of Violence,* 1965. University of California, Berkeley, California. Boulding, Kenneth E.: *Conflict and Defense,* 1963. Harper and Row, New York, New York.

Bullowa, Margaret: *Before Speech: The Beginning of Interpersonal Communication,* 1979. Cambridge University Press, Cambridge, Massachusetts.

Burgoon, Judee K. and Saine, Thomas: *The Unspoken Dialogue—An Introduction to Non-verbal Communication,* 1928. Houghton Mifflin Company, New York, New York.

Coffin, Royce A.: *The Negotiator: A Manual for Winners,* 1973. Amacon, New York, New York.

Coser, Lewis: *The Function of Social Conflict,* 1956. Free Press, New York, New York.

Curle, Adam, *Making Peace,* 1971. Barnes and Noble, New York, New York.

Dahrendorf, Ralph: *Class and Class Conflict in Industrial Society,* 1959. Stanford University Press, Stanford, California.

Davis, Martha: *Understanding Body Movement: An Annotated Bibliography,* 1972. Arno Press, Salem, New Hampshire.

Deutsch, Morton: *The Resolution of Conflict,* 1973. Yale University Press, New Haven, Connecticut.

Dubois, Rachael and Li, Soo M.: *Reducing Social Tension and Conflict,* 1972. Associated Press, New York.

Elkouri, Frank and Elkouri, Edna Asper: *How Arbitration Works,* 1960. Bureau of National Affairs, Washington, D.C.

Evarts, W. Richard et al: "The Mediation of Intellectual Property Disputes." Proceedings of the Patent Law Institute. Matthew Bender (Southwestern Legal Academy), 1983.

Fast, Julius: *Body Language,* 1970. M. Evans, New York, New York.

Feinburg, Joel: *Social Philosophy,* 1973. Prentice Hall, Englewood Cliffs, New Jersey.

Filley, Alan: *Interpersonal Conflict Resolution,* 1975. Scott Foresman and Company, Glenview, Illinois.

Fisher, Roger: *International Conflict for Beginners,* 1979. Harper Colophon Books, New York, New York.

Fisher, Roger: *International Mediation: A Working Guide,* 1978. International Peace Academy, New York, New York.

Frankena, William K.: *Ethics,* 1973. Prentice Hall, Englewood Cliffs, New Jersey.

Frost, Joyce Hocker and Wilmot, William. *Interpersonal Conflict,* 1978. Wm. C. Brown Company Publishers, Dubuque, Iowa.

Gibb, Jack R.: *Trust: A New View of Personal and Organizational Development,* 1978. Guild of Tutors Press, Los Angeles, California.

Greenstone, James L.: "Marriage and Family Crisis." *Emotional First Aid: A Journal of Crisis Intervention,* 1978. American Academy of Crisis Interveners, Louisville, Kentucky.

Greenstone, James L. and Leviton, Sharon C.: *The Crisis Intervener's Handbook,* Volume I, 1979. Crisis Management Workshops, Dallas, Texas.

Greenstone, James L. and Leviton, Sharon C.: *The Crisis Interveners Handbook, Volume II,* 1980. Rothschild Publishing House, Dallas, Texas.

Greenstone, James L. and Leviton, Sharon C.: "Crisis Management: A Basic Concern." *The Crisis Intervener's Newsletter,* 1980. Southwestern Academy of Crisis Interveners, Dallas, Texas.

Greenstone, James L. and Leviton, Sharon C.: *Crisis Management and Intervener Survival,* 1979. Affective House, Tulsa, Oklahoma.

Greenstone, James L. and Leviton, Sharon C.: "Crisis Intervention and Intervener Survival." In Raymond Corsini (Ed) *Innovative Psychotherapies,* 1981. John Wiley Interscience, New York, New York.

Greenstone, James L. and Leviton, Sharon C.: *Hotline: Crisis Intervention Directory,* 1981. Facts on File, New York, New York.

Grinder, John: *Frogs Into Princes: Neuro-Linguistic Programming,* 1979. Real People, Moab, Utah.

Gulliver, P. H.: *Disputes and Negotiations: A Cross Cultural Approach,* 1979. Academic Press, New York, New York.

Harrison, Randall P.: *Beyond Words,* 1974. Prentice-Hall, Englewood Cliffs, New Jersey.

Hersey, Paul, and Blanchard, Kenneth: *Management of Organizational Behavior:* Utilizing Human Resources, 1972. Prentice-Hall, Englewood Cliffs, New Jersey.

Hobbs, Thomas: *Leviathan;* ed. by C. B. Macpherson, 1975. Penguin Books, New York, New York.

Jandt, Fred: *Conflict Resolution Through Communication,* 1973. Harper and Row, New York, New York.

Kahn, Robert L.; and Boulding, Kenneth E., eds.: *Power and Conflict in Organizations,* 1964. Basic Books, New York, New York.

Karass, Chester L.: *The Negotiating Game,* 1970. Thomas Y. Crowell Company, New York, New York.

Kessler, Sheila: *Creative Conflict Resolution: Mediation,* 1978. National Institute for Professional Training, Atlanta, Georgia.

Kissinger, Henry: *Works Restored: Politics of Conservatism in a Revolutionary Age,* 1964. Grossett & Dunlap, New York, New York.

Klenke, Chris L.: *First Impressions,* 1975, Prentice Hall, Englewood Cliffs, New Jersey.

Knapp, Mark: *Essentials of Nonverbal Communication,* 1980. Holt, Rinehart and Wilson, New York, New York.

Kriesberg, Louis: *Sociology of Social Conflict,* 1973. Prentice Hall, Englewood Cliffs, New Jersey.

LaFrance, Marianne: *Moving Bodies: Non-verbal Communication in Social Relationships,* 1978. Brooks/Cole Publishing Company, Monterey, California.

Lee, Linda: Handbook: *Interpreting Handshakes, Gestures, Signals and Sexual Signs,* 1980. Prentice Hall, Englewood Cliffs, New Jersey.

Leviton, Sharon C.: *A Practical Guide to Crisis Intervention,* 1983. Dissertation published by Southeastern University, New Orleans, Louisiana.

Likert, Rensis; and Likert, Jane Gibson: *New Ways of Managing Conflict,* 1976. McGraw-Hill, New York, New York.

Lorenz, Konrad: *On Aggression,* 1969. Bantum, New York, New York.

Nierenberg, Gerard I.: *Fundamentals of Negotiating,* 1973. W. Clement Stone, Publishers, New York.

Nierenberg, Gerard I.; *How to Read a Person Like a Book,* 1971. Hawthorn Books, New York, New York.

Parad, H. J., Resnik, H. L. P., Ruben, H. L., Zusman, J. and Ruben, Diane D.: "Crisis Intervention and Emergency Mental Health Care: Concepts and Principles." In Resnik, H. L. P. and Ruben, H. L. (Eds.) *Emergency Psychiatric Care,* 1975. Charles Press Publishers, Bowie, Maryland.

Pelton, Leroy, *Psychology of Nonviolence,* 1974. Porgamon, Elmspond, New York.

Prince, George M.: *The Practice of Creativity,* 1970. Harper and Row, New York, New York.

Rosenbluh, Edward S.: *Techniques of Crisis Intervention,* 1974. Behavioral Science Service, Louisville, Kentucky.

Sartorium, Rolf E.: *Individual Conduct and Social Norms,* 1975. Dickerson Publishing Company.

Spiegal, John Paul: *Messages of the Body,* 1974. Free Press, New York, New York.

Thomson, David S.; *Language,* 1975. Time/Life Books, Alexandria, Virginia.

Walton, Richard E.: *Interpersonal Peacemaking: Confrontations and Third-Party Consultation,* 1969. Addison-Wesley, Reading, Massachusetts.

Wehr, Paul: *Conflict Regulation,* 1979. Westview Press, Boulder, Colorado.

Weitz, Shirley; *Nonverbal Communication: Readings With Commentary;* 2nd edition, 1979. Oxford University Press, New York, New York.

Articles

"Help, Not Hassle, Dispute Resolution Centers: the Nation's Newest Growth Industry," in the American Bar Association Journal, January, 1983.

"The Mini-Hearing: An Alternative to Protracted Litigation of Factually Complex Disputes," in the American Bar Association Business Lawyer, November, 1982.

"Corporate Dispute Management," 1983. Published by the Center for Public Resources, New York City, New York.

W. Richard Evarts is the Executive Director of the Dispute Mediation Service of Dallas, Texas, and he previously served as the Executive Director of the Center for Dispute Resolution in Denver, Colorado. He holds a Masters degree from the American University, is the founder of *The Journal of Interpersonal Conflict Management,* and is the author of a number of papers on dispute mediation. He is a member of the American Arbitration Association and the National Academy of Conciliators.

Dr. James L. Greenstone has been a Marriage and Family Psychotherapist since 1966 and is the President of the Southwest Academy of Crisis Intervention in Dallas, Texas. He is also Chairman of the American Board of Examiners in Crisis Intervention and National Vice-President of the American Academy of Crisis Intervention. He is certified as a Mediator by the Dispute Mediation Service of Dallas and is Senior Editor of *Emotional First Aid: A Journal of Crisis Intervention.* He has co-authored a chapter on conflict mediation in *The Wiley Encyclopedia of Psychology,* edited by Raymond Corsisi, John Wiley & Sons 1983. He has also co-authored the books, *Hotline: Crisis Intervention Directory,* Facts On File 1981, and *Crisis Intervention: A Handbook for Mediators,* Kendall/Hunt Publishing Co. 1982.

Gary J. Kirkpatrick is a member of the staff of Dispute Mediation Service of Dallas and previously served as a Criminal Justice System Liasion with the Center for Dispute Resolution in Denver, Colorado. He holds a Bachelors degree from the University of Colorado and is certified as a Mediator by the National Academy of Concilitors.

Dr. Sharon C. Leviton is a practicing psychotherapist and Executive Director of the Southwestern Academy of Crisis Intervention. She is a Diplomate of the American Board of Examiners in Crisis Intervention and a certified Mediator of the Dispute Mediation Service of Dallas. She has co-authored a chapter on conflict mediation in *The Wiley Encyclopedia of Psychology,* edited by Raymond Corsisi, John Wiley & Sons 1983. She has also co-authored the books, *Hotline: Crisis Intervention Directory,* Facts on File 1981, and *Crisis Intervention: A Handbook for Mediators,* Kendall/Hunt Publishing Co. 1982.